ANNIE SUSSEL

Agrégée de l'Université

L'anglais au baccalauréat

FAIRE LE POINT

CLASSIQUES HACHETTE

Dans la même collection (extraits du catalogue) :

S. Auroux et Y. Weil.
Nouveau vocabulaire des études philosophiques
Dictionnaire des auteurs et des thèmes de la philosophie

R. Blanchard et M. Hémeret.
Le problème de physique au baccalauréat

Bautran-Vento.
Exercices résolus de physique pour les :
Terminales C, E

R. Blanchard, M. Hémeret et J. Gougeon.
La question de cours de sciences physiques au baccalauréat

J.-L. Liters et C. Tchigique.
Exercices résolus de mathématiques :
Algèbre, Terminales C, E
Analyse, Terminales B, C, D, E
Géométrie, Terminales C, E
Algèbre et géométrie, Terminale D
Probabilités et statistiques, 1re et Terminales

C. J. Bertrand et C. Lévy.
L'anglais de base

C. Chatelanat et T. Henzi.
Vocabulaire de base allemand-français

J. Chassard et G. Weil.
Dictionnaire des œuvres et des thèmes de la littérature allemande

J. Chassard et G. Weil.
L'épreuve d'allemand au baccalauréat

Collection FEU VERT — Série RAS :

BAC — Sujets commentés :
Français (séries A, B, C, D, E)
Français (séries F, G, H)
Philosophie
Mathématiques (séries A et B)
Mathématiques (série D)
Mathématiques (séries C et E)
Physique (série D)
Physique (séries C et E)
Anglais (série A)
Biologie (série D)
Économie (série B)

Sujets seuls :
Mathématiques (séries C et E)
Mathématiques (série D)

CLASSIQUES HACHETTE

La loi du 11 mars 1957 n'autorisant, aux termes des alinéas 2 et 3 de l'article 41 d'une part, que les « copies ou reproductions strictement réservées à l'usage privé du copiste et non destinées à une utilisation collective », et, d'autre part, que les analyses et les courtes citations dans un but d'exemple et d'illustration, « toute reproduction ou reproduction intégrale ou partielle, faite sans le consentement de l'auteur ou de ses ayants droit ou ayants cause, est illicite » (alinéa 1er de l'article 40). Cette représentation ou reproduction par quelque procédé que ce soit, constituerait donc une contrefaçon sanctionnée par les articles 425 et suivants du Code pénal.

I.S.B.N. 2.01.003029.X
© 1976 LIBRAIRIE HACHETTE
Tous droits de traduction,
de reproduction et d'adaptation
réservés pour tous pays.

Comment utiliser cet aide-mémoire

Cet aide-mémoire se propose d'aider les candidats qui présentent l'anglais au baccalauréat à revoir quelques notions essentielles de civilisation des États-Unis d'une part, de vocabulaire et de grammaire d'autre part.

Chaque chapitre se compose donc de deux parties :

1 / Civilisation et vocabulaire

Sur la page de gauche, un texte donne les indications de base que tout candidat doit connaître.
Face à ce texte, le candidat trouvera la traduction des mots et expressions qu'il pourrait avoir du mal à comprendre immédiatement, ceci afin de lui permettre une lecture suivie.
De plus, nous avons cru bon, dans certains cas, de compléter ce vocabulaire par certains mots et expressions que le candidat pourra éventuellement utiliser pour son explication de texte, à l'oral. Enfin, pour chaque terme ou membre de phrase, nous avons indiqué en caractère gras la syllabe ou les syllabes accentuées, dont l'ignorance est si souvent à l'origine d'une prononciation authentiquement... française !

2 / Grammaire

Après s'être remis en mémoire la règle ou les règles indiquées sur la page de gauche, le candidat pourra faire les exercices proposés sur la page de droite. Le test qui se trouve à la fin de chaque chapitre lui permettra de s'assurer qu'il a assimilé les notions de grammaire.
Puis, s'il le souhaite, il s'exercera à la traduction à l'aide des quelques thèmes qui se trouvent aux dernières pages de chaque chapitre.
Pour tous les exercices, des corrigés sont donnés à la fin du livre.

Nous espérons que ce petit livre facilitera les révisions des candidats au baccalauréat.
Nous remercions très sincèrement nos collègues et amis qui ont bien voulu nous aider.
Nous accueillerons avec reconnaissance les remarques et les critiques de nos lecteurs, et d'avance nous les en remercions.

Expressions utiles pour le commentaire de texte

Ce texte traite de...	This text deals with...
	This text is about...
Ce texte nous informe sur...	This text acquaints us with...
Ce texte est une analyse exacte de la situation.	This text is an accurate analysis of the situation.
L'auteur y insiste sur...	The author { concentrates upon... / lays the emphasis upon...
Il montre une grande connaissance du problème.	He shows great insight into the problem.
Il a de bonnes raisons d'affirmer ceci.	He has good grounds for saying this.
Son but est de convaincre...	He aims at convincing...
En dépit de ce qu'affirme l'auteur...	In spite of (= Despite = Notwithstanding) the author's assertion...
Il enfonce des portes ouvertes.	He states the obvious.
Je vais tout à fait dans le sens de l'auteur.	I fully agree with the author.
Cependant...	However = Nevertheless = Yet...
Nous devons nous abstenir de...	We must refrain from + GERUND
Selon ce texte...	According to this text...
Apparemment...	Apparently = Seemingly...
En fait...	In fact = Actually...
L'auteur laisse entendre que...	The author intimates that...
Alors que...	Whereas...
Nous ne devons pas oublier que...	We must bear in mind that...
Le plus souvent...	In most cases = more often than not...
Il ne faut pas aller trop loin...	We must not go too far...
Nous devons aller plus loin...	We must go further...

EXPRESSIONS UTILES

Nous pouvons aller jusqu'à dire...	We may go as far as to say...
Si je puis dire, en quelque sorte...	As it were...
En d'autres termes...	In other words...
Donc, par conséquent	Therefore, consequently
A cet égard...	In this respect = in this connexion...
En ce qui concerne...	As to = Regarding...
De plus...	Moreover = furthermore = besides = in addition
D'une part... d'autre part...	On the one hand... on the other hand...
Ceci n'est qu'un exemple... Ceci peut servir d'exemple...	This is but an example... This may serve as an example...
Nous pouvons nous demander si...	We may wonder if...
Je ne veux pas dire que...	I do not mean that = I am not intimating that...
Sans aucun doute	Undoubtedly = No doubt
Aussi étrange que cela puisse paraître...	Strange as it may seem...
En tout cas...	At any rate = in any case
Au contraire...	On the contrary...
Il s'ensuit que...	It follows that...
On pourrait dire que...	One could argue that...
Nous pouvons déduire de ce que dit l'auteur que...	We may infer from what the author says that...
En conclusion...	In conclusion...

1 The Indians

Before the arrival of the Europeans, America was inhabited by people belonging to the yellow race. Their complexion was of a reddish-brown hue. The Europeans called them Indians or Redskins.

1 The Indians before the arrival of the Europeans

Many different tribes lived on the American territory. At the beginning, almost all of them were engaged in agricultural activities. This is still the case with the Indians of the southwest: the Pueblo Indians.
But in the 17th and 18th centuries, after the horse had been imported into Mexico by the Spaniards, some tribes based their way of life on buffalo hunting.
The tribes were under the authority of chiefs. The chiefs were chosen for their abilities as warriors for the tribes were often at war with one another.

2 The relations between the Indians and the Palefaces

As long as colonization was limited, the conflicts were also limited. But in the 19th century they became more cruel with the spread of colonization and the increasing reduction of the Indians' hunting-grounds by the American authorities. In order to wipe out some tribes, the Palefaces killed even women and children.
The resistance of the Indians ceased at the end of the 19th century with the surrenders of Cochise and Geronimo, the death of Sitting Bull and the massacre of Wounded Knee in 1890.

3 The Indians today

Hardly more than half a million Indians live in the U.S. today. Some of them live on reservations, others have adjusted to modern civilization: for instance, construction-workers and window-cleaners for the skyscrapers are recruited among the Mohawks who are not subject to vertigo...
Over the past few years movements have arisen, particularly among the younger Indians. They demand a better status, or even independence for their people.
The attitude of the Americans towards the Indians is ambiguous, as is testified by the cinema. It is often racist and influenced by a guilty conscience.

THE MAKING OF AMERICA

inhabited (1)	habité
complexion	teint
hue	couleur, ton
the Redskins	les Peaux-Rouges

1

a tribe	une tribu
to be engaged in	se livrer à (une activité)
the Spaniards	les Espagnols
buffalo (2)	U.S.: bison
hunting	la chasse
abilities	capacités
a warrior	un guerrier

2

the Palefaces	les Visages Pâles
as long as	tant que
spread	extension
hunting-grounds	terrains de chasse
to wipe out	exterminer
surrender	reddition

3

hardly	à peine
a reservation	une réserve
to adjust to	s'adapter à
a construction-worker	un charpentier, un ouvrier du bâtiment
a window-cleaner	un laveur de carreaux
a skyscraper	un gratte-ciel
to be subject to	être sujet à
vertigo	le vertige
over the past few years	au cours de ces dernières années
to arise (arose, arisen)	apparaître, naître
to demand (3)	réclamer, exiger
status	statut
as is testified by	comme le montre bien
a guilty conscience	mauvaise conscience

OTHER WORDS AND PHRASES

---

cabin	hutte, case
tent, tepee	tente, tepee
basket weaving	la vannerie
pottery	la poterie
the medicine man	le sorcier des Indiens
to dig up the hatchet	déterrer la hache de guerre
to bury the hatchet	enterrer la hache de guerre
to smoke the peace pipe	fumer le calumet de la paix
a bow	un arc
a quiver	un carquois
an arrow	une flèche
a feather head-dress	une coiffure de plumes

---

1. Inhabité se dit : **uninhabited.**
2. G.B. : **buffalo** : buffle; **bison** : bison.
3. Faux-ami ! demander : **to ask.**

2 Colonial America

1 The first settlers
Towards the end of the 16th century the first European immigrants settled down on the territories which were to become the United States.

In 1620 the *Pilgrim Fathers* arrived with the *Mayflower*. They were English Calvinists who wanted to be free to practise their religion.

In the 17th and 18th centuries most immigrants went to America for political or religious reasons. However there were already poor farmers who migrated to America in the hope of making a new start on this new continent.

2 The North and the South
Two types of civilization soon emerged.

In the North most of the settlers were rather impecunious people who tilled the land with the help of their families and and a few farm-hands.

In the South the big plantations belonged to members of rich English families. They were cultivated by black slaves imported from Africa.

In the North, where people and manners were uncouth, great opportunities rewarded individual enterprise. On the contrary, the South enjoyed a refined civilization, but it was based on slavery.

3 The Thirteen Colonies
By the middle of the 18th century, the English territories consisted of thirteen colonies which were all located on the Atlantic coast. They were peopled by about one and a half million inhabitants.

Though the Governor was the representative of the King of England, his salary as well as the local taxes were fixed by local councils.

But the King of England levied customs duties on all goods entering or leaving America.

The economy of the Thirteen Colonies was in full growth. They no longer had anything to fear from the two powers which had traditionally opposed English influence in America: France and Spain.

THE MAKING OF AMERICA

1

a **set**tler	un colon
to **set**tle **down**	s'installer
which **were** to be**come**	qui devaient devenir
the **Pil**grim **Fa**thers	les Pères Pèlerins
al**rea**dy	déjà
to **make** a **new start**	prendre un nouveau départ

2

to e**merge**	apparaître
impe**cu**nious	besogneux, impécunieux
to **till** the **land**	cultiver la terre
a **farm**-hand	un journalier, un manouvrier
to be**long** to	appartenir à
un**couth**	rude, grossier
an **op**portu**ni**ty	une occasion favorable
slavery	l'esclavage

3

lo**ca**ted	situé
as **well** as	ainsi que
a **tax**	un impôt
to **le**vy (**tax**es, **du**ties)	lever (des impôts, des droits)
customs **du**ties	taxes douanières
goods	marchandises
growth	développement, croissance

OTHER WORDS AND PHRASES
---

hardships	difficultés
a **rough cross**ing	une traversée (maritime) difficile
to **found** (a **vil**lage, a **state**)	fonder (1)
to **clear** the **land** for **cul**ti**va**tion	défricher la terre
by **dint** of **hard work**	à force de travailler dur
to **work** with **all** one's **might**	travailler de toutes ses forces
to **grow** (to**bac**co, **cot**ton, **rice**, **in**digo, etc...)	cultiver (le tabac, le coton, le riz, l'indigo, etc...)
to **gath**er (**cot**ton, etc...)	cueillir (le coton, etc...)
a **back-break**ing task	un travail éreintant
a **Nor**therner	un habitant du Nord (2)
a **Sou**therner	un habitant du Sud (2)
a **lei**surely **way** of **life**	une vie oisive
a **log-ca**bin	une cabane de pionnier (faite de rondins)

---

1. Ne pas confondre ce verbe régulier avec le prétérit et le participe passé de **to find (found, found)**: trouver.
2. Ne pas traduire par **Sudiste** ou **Nordiste**, termes réservés aux combattants de la Guerre de Sécession.

3 Independence war

1 The causes of the war

After it had defeated the French in Canada (1763), the English government was faced with financial difficulties resulting from the war expenses.
In order to refill the coffers of the state, the government set very high customs duties on products which were essential to the inhabitants of the Thirteen colonies. Moreover, stronger measures were taken against smugglers.
In addition to all this, by the Stamp Act, the English government fixed a new tax levied on all British subjects.
The American colonists refused to pay this tax. The King of England abolished it but he created other taxes and took measures that bore unjustly upon American merchants.
The exasperation of the Americans was such that, in Boston, in December 1773, demonstrators dressed as Indians threw overboard a cargo of tea that had been brought from England (Boston Tea Party).
This marked the end of the relations between England and America.

2 The war

On July 4, 1776, the Thirteen colonies declared their independence. A Congress gathered in Philadelphia proclaimed the birth of a new state: the United States of America.
England refused to recognize the new state and war broke out. The war lasted from 1776 to 1783. Under the command of George Washington the Insurgents at first suffered set-backs. But in February 1778, the French government, anxious to get its revenge on England, signed a treaty of alliance with the United States and sent expeditionary forces to America. The English troops of General Cornwallis had to fall back. Surrounded by the troops of Washington and Lafayette and the ships of de Grasse, Cornwallis capitulated in October 1781.

3 The United States of America

In November 1782, the English recognized the independence of the United States.
But it was not before 1789 that the new state began to work normally when the Constitution passed in 1787 came into operation. The first president of the United States was George Washington.

THE MAKING OF AMERICA

1

to de**feat**	vaincre
to re**sult** from (1)	provenir de
war expenses	dépenses de guerre
in **or**der to	afin de
the **cof**fers of the **state**	les coffres de l'État
to **set** a **du**ty, a **tax**	fixer un droit, un impôt
es**sen**tial to	indispensable à
more**o**ver	de plus
smug**g**lers	contrebandiers
in ad**di**tion to	en plus de
to **bear** un**just**ly u**pon**	être défavorable à
a **de**monstrator	un manifestant
overboard	par-dessus bord
a **car**go	une cargaison

2

war broke out	la guerre éclata
to **last**	durer
under the com**mand** of	sous le commandement de
to **suf**fer **set**-backs	subir des revers
anxious to	désireux de
to **fall back**	se replier

3

to **come** into **o**peration	être appliqué(e) (loi, mesure)

OTHER WORDS AND PHRASES

a re**bell**ion	une révolte
a **ri**ot	une émeute
a **de**mons**tra**tion	une manifestation
an in**sur**gent	un rebelle, un insurgé
a **Lo**yalist	un Loyaliste (Américain fidèle à la couronne d'Angleterre)
a **Pa**triot	un Patriote (Américain partisan de l'Indépendance)
the **Red Coats**	les fantassins anglais
Inde**pen**dence Day	la fête nationale américaine (4 juillet)
tarred and **fea**thered	passé au goudron et roulé dans les plumes (punition des Loyalistes)
to de**clare war** u**pon**	déclarer la guerre à
to **be** at **war** with	être en guerre contre
to **wage war**	faire la guerre
to **suf**fer **ca**sualties	subir des pertes
wounded	blessé
maimed	mutilé
to be**siege**	assiéger
to en**cir**cle	encercler
the **van**quished	les vaincus
a **rout**	une déroute
a **truce**	une trêve
a **peace** treaty	un traité de paix

---

1. Ne pas confondre avec **to result in**: aboutir à.

4 The Frontier

1 The Frontier

During the first half of the 19th century the territory of the U.S. was enlarged by several accretions: Louisiana (purchased from the French) and vast tracts of land in the South (won from Mexico).

Moreover the region stretching from the Mississippi to the Rocky Mountains was being gradually explored.

Originally those territories were practically uninhabited. But the wide stretches of new land attracted all those who had been driven away from Europe by political persecution or destitution. By mid-century there were more than 200 000 immigrants every year.

Between 1830 and 1860 the population of the U.S. rose from 13 to 31 million inhabitants.

The Frontier, that is to say the moving line between cultivated and waste land, was pushed westwards.

2 The Pioneer Spirit

The first pioneers were mostly farmers who settled down on the lands between the Appalachians and the Rockies, cleared them, sowed grain, then bought the land at a low price from the federal government.

Those pioneers often sold their land a little later and moved further west.

The rough hard life of the pioneers, their taste for individual freedom, their interest in local matters rather than in national politics were to leave their stamp on the history of the U.S..

3 Going West

Originally the immigrant industrial workers remained in the ports of the East coast.

But with the development of industry based upon Pennsylvania coal, the Gold Rush to California, the development of railways and the construction of canals, industrial towns appeared in the new regions.

By the middle of the 19th century, there were two entirely different kinds of states in the U.S.:

a/ the Eastern and Frontier states, which based their prosperity upon owner farming, industry and the Pioneer Spirit;

b/ the Southern states, which clung to a colonialist way of life based upon slavery.

THE MAKING OF AMERICA

1

the **Fron**tier	la « Frontière » (front pionnier) (1)
ac**cre**tions	acquisitions
to **pur**chase	acheter
a **tract** of **land**	une étendue de terre
won from	conquis sur
more**o**ver	de plus
stretching	qui s'étend
originally	au début
a **stretch** of **land**	une étendue de terre
to be **driv**en a**way**	être chassé
desti**tu**tion	la misère
by **mid**-**cen**tury	au milieu du siècle
waste land	région en friche
westwards	en direction de l'ouest

2

pio**neer**	pionnier
the **Rock**ies = the **Rock**y **Mount**ains	les Rocheuses
to **clear** the **land**	défricher la terre
to **sow** (sowed, sown)	semer
rough	rude
to **leave** one's **stamp** u**pon**	marquer

3

an in**dus**trial **work**er	un ouvrier de l'industrie
owner **farm**ing	le faire-valoir direct (2)
to **cling** (**clung**, **clung**) to	rester attaché à

OTHER WORDS AND PHRASES

a **wag**gon	un chariot
to **fell trees**	abattre des arbres
to **plough** the **land**	labourer la terre
to be **self**-**reli**ant	1/ être indépendant 2/ avoir confiance en soi
a **gold**-digger	un chercheur d'or
a **gold nug**get	une pépite
a **pick**	une pioche
a **sho**vel	une pelle
a **sieve**	un tamis

---

1. Frontière (entre deux pays) : **border(-line)**.
2. Exploitation de la terre par son propriétaire.

5 The Civil War

1 The North versus the South

For a long time there had been a clash of interests between the North and the South.

An ideal of individual freedom and free enterprise prevailed in the North with the small farmers and the manufacturers. In the South the aristocratic notions of the great property owners whose black slaves cultivated the land were deep-rooted.

The North believed in protectionist customs tariffs whereas the South was all for free-trade.

The conflict crystallized around slavery: would there be slaves in the territories of the West where new states were being created? Could slavery survive in the South?

2 The conflict

The conflict broke out after the election of President Abraham Lincoln who was an abolitionist.

In 1861, South Carolina left the Union. It was followed by ten Southern states.

In April 1861, the Civil War broke out. There were 23 million Northerners against 9 million Southerners, half of whom were slaves. The North enjoyed an overwhelming superiority in armaments, railways and ships.

However the South held out for four years.

In April 1865, General Lee, the leader of the Confederates, surrendered to General Grant in Appomatox.

3 The consequences of the Civil War

The war led to the emancipation of the Blacks.

Its cost in human lives was high: 600 000 dead.

The South was devastated: the houses had been destroyed, the factories ransacked, the cotton fields laid waste.

In the years that followed, the South was exploited by the carpet-baggers: they were political and financial adventurers who had come from the North.

Yet the social structure of the South was but little changed. The Blacks, who had become farm-hands, were still entirely dependent upon the planters who still owned the land.

The scene was set for the development of the Black problem. The Ku Klux Klan, whose aim was to prevent the Blacks from exercising their political rights, was organized as early as 1867.

THE MAKING OF AMERICA

the **Civil War**	la Guerre de Sécession

1

versus	contre
a **clash** of **in**terests	un conflit d'intérêts
to pre**vail**	prédominer
a **manufac**turer	un industriel
deep-**root**ed	profondément enraciné
customs **ta**riffs	tarifs douaniers
where**as**	tandis que (1)
to be **all** for	tenir à
free-**trade**	le libre échange
crystallized	se cristallisa

2

to **break out**	éclater
an **abol**itionist	un antiesclavagiste
a **Nor**therner	1/ un habitant du Nord 2/ un Nordiste (2)
over**whelm**ing	écrasant
to **hold out**	tenir, résister
the Con**fe**derates	les Confédérés (2)

3

to **lead** (led, led) to	entraîner
cost	coût
devastated	ravagé
ransacked	saccagé
laid waste	dévasté
a **car**pet-**bag**ger	un "carpet-bagger" (3)

an ad**ven**turer	un aventurier
was but **little changed**	ne fut que fort peu changée
to be de**pend**ent u**pon**	dépendre de
to **own**	posséder
an **aim**	un but
to pre**vent**	empêcher
to **ex**ercise one's **rights**	exercer ses droits
as **ear**ly as	dès

OTHER WORDS AND PHRASES

the **Whigs**	les représentants politiques du Nord
the **De**mocrats	les représentants politiques du Sud
the **Yank**ees (= the **Yanks**)	les Nordistes
to se**cede**	faire sécession
to be out**num**bered	être inférieur en nombre
to out**num**ber	être supérieur en nombre
the **Re**con**struc**tion	la période qui suivit la guerre

---

1. Exprime l'opposition entre deux faits et non la durée **(while)**.
2. Vocabulaire réservé à la Guerre de Sécession.
3. Aventurier qui arrivait du Nord en n'apportant qu'une petite valise de tapisserie **(carpet-bag)**. Le terme est donc très spécialisé et réservé à cette époque de l'histoire des États-Unis.

6 The Melting-pot

There were 31 million Americans in 1860, 76 million in 1900. Though the birthrate was high, this tremendous increase was due mainly to immigration.
Immigration had been facilitated by improved sea transport (shorter voyages, cheaper fares) and by an increasing demand for agricultural and industrial manpower.

1 The Melting-pot
Until 1885 most immigrants were of English, Scottish, Irish, German or Scandinavian descent. They were easily integrated. At the end of the century, however, there came new immigrants with a different background. They came mostly from Eastern Europe (Russians, Poles, Czechs) or Mediterranean Europe (Greeks and Italians).
At that time also the American Jewish community was formed. Most of the Jewish immigrants came from the western regions of the Russian Empire.
Those newcomers were rejected by the American community and this was expressed, at the beginning of the 20th century, in the *Immigration Acts*.
As to the manufacturers of the East coast, they were glad to employ this unskilled but cheap labour. The women in particular worked in the sweat-shops to the utmost of their strength.

2 The American Dream
In spite of the hardships met with by the newcomers, the number of believers in the "American Dream" kept rising. All dreamt of religious and political freedom, of better living conditions, and possibly of being rich one day. A few generations later, the descendants of these immigrants had been integrated. The American melting-pot, or crucible, had melted them down and produced the average American.

3 The Melting-pot in question
Some American sociologists nowadays lay the emphasis upon the social privileges still enjoyed by the WASPs (White Anglo-Saxon Protestants).
Others stress the original cultural traits which have been preserved by some and which they consider as part of the American cultural heritage as a whole.

THE MAKING OF AMERICA

the **melt**ing-pot = the **cru**cible	le creuset	a **sweat**-shop	un atelier où les ouvriers sont exploités
the **birth**rate	le taux de natalité	to the **ut**most of	jusqu'à l'extrême limite de
tre**men**dous	énorme		
to be **due** to	être dû à (1)	**2**	
mainly	surtout		
im**proved**	amélioré	the American **Dream**	le Rêve américain
a **voy**age (2)	un voyage par mer	in **spite** of	malgré, en dépit de
cheap	bon marché	a **hard**ship	une épreuve
the **fare**	le prix du voyage	**kept ri**sing	continua d'augmenter
in**creas**ing	croissant(e)	to **melt down**	fondre
manpower = **labour**	main-d'œuvre	**av**erage	moyen

1

to be of **Eng**lish de**scent**	être d'origine anglaise
integrated	assimilé
how**ev**er	cependant
there **came**	il vint
the **back**ground	l'environnement social
Eastern **Eu**rope	l'Europe centrale
a **Pole**	un Polonais (3)
a **Czech**	un Tchèque (3)
Jewish	juif (adjectif) (4)
a **new**comer	un nouveau-venu
the Immi**gra**tion **Acts**	les lois sur l'immigration (5)
as to	quant à / aux
unskilled	non qualifié

3

in **quest**ion	contesté
nowadays	de nos jours, aujourd'hui
to **lay** the **em**phasis u**pon**	mettre l'accent sur
privileges en**joyed** by	les privilèges dont jouissent
to pre**serve**	conserver
as a **whole**	dans son ensemble

---

1. Attention ! La construction **to be due to** peut avoir un sens très différent. **He is due to arrive early**: il doit arriver de bonne heure.
2. Terme réservé au voyage maritime. Un voyage : **a journey, a trip**.
3. Adjectifs : **Polish, Czech**.
4. Nom : **a Jew** (un Juif).
5. Lois favorisant l'entrée d'immigrants d'origine anglo-saxonne et protestante.

7 The Crisis of 1929 and the New Deal

Because they were the suppliers of Europe, the United States substantially developed their economy during the first World War. After the war, they entered the Prosperity Era.

1 The Prosperity Era

Though agriculture stagnated, the American economy throve for a decade (1918-1928).

Industry prospered and mergers led to the formation of many trusts.

A wave of intensive speculation reached large sections of the population.

But, in fact, the actual industrial growth did not correspond to the speculation. As early as 1928 the slump was looming large.

This period was also the era of prohibition and of the bootleggers.

2 The Crisis

On October 24, 1929 (Black Thursday), the quotations of the shares on the Stock Exchange collapsed.

The banks stopped their payments, the factories closed down. The number of unemployed workers reached 12 million in 1933. The Republicans, who had been in power since 1921, proved unable to get the crisis under control. Hoover being then President, it became common to use the derisive term *Hoovervilles* for the shantytowns where the poor and the unemployed lived. Therefore, in November 1932, the Democratic candidate, F. D. Roosevelt, was elected President.

3 The New Deal

In pursuance of the doctrines of the English economist, Lord Keynes, Roosevelt and his collaborators applied a policy of government spending to boost the economy. This policy was defined by Roosevelt as the New Deal.

Roosevelt had to face the opposition of the conservative spheres and of the Supreme Court, but he overruled it. However, it was only in 1938 that the economic recovery became tangible. And it was only with World War II that the United States, which resumed its role as supplier of Europe, was able finally to overcome the economic crisis.

the **New Deal**	la Nouvelle Donne
a sup**pli**er	un fournisseur
sub**stan**tially	considérablement
an **e**ra	une ère

1

to stag**nate**	stagner
to **thrive** (**throve**, **thri**ven)	prospérer, être florissant
a **de**cade	une décennie
to **pros**per	prospérer
a **mer**ger	une fusion
a **wave**	une vague
to **reach**	toucher, atteindre
actual	réel (1)
growth	croissance
a **slump**	une crise économique
to **loom large**	menacer de façon imminente
a **boot**legger	un contrebandier ou un vendeur de boissons alcoolisées prohibées

2

Black Thursday	le Jeudi Noir
a quo**ta**tion on the **Stock Ex**change	une cotation en bourse
to col**lapse**	s'effondrer
un**em**ployed	au chômage
to **prove** unable	se montrer incapable
to **get** sth. **un**der con**trol**	maîtriser qch.
deri**sive**	ironique
a **shan**tytown	un bidonville

3

in pur**sua**nce of	conformément à
to ap**ply**	appliquer
a **po**licy	une politique
government **spend**ing	dépenses publiques
to **boost**	relancer
the con**ser**vative **spheres**	les milieux conservateurs
the Su**preme** Court	la Cour Suprême
to over**rule** sth.	passer outre à qch.
the eco**no**mic re**co**very	le redressement économique
tangible	sensible, manifeste
to re**sume** a **role**	reprendre un rôle
to over**come**	surmonter

OTHER WORDS AND PHRASES

Hoover **flags**	les poches retournées des chômeurs et des pauvres
a **speak-ea**sy	endroit où l'on vendait des boissons alcoolisées prohibées
the **dole**	l'indemnité de chômage
to be in a **sor**ry pre**di**cament	être dans une triste situation
to be unable to **make both ends meet**	ne pas pouvoir joindre les deux bouts
to **live** from **hand** to **mouth**	vivre au jour le jour

---

1. Faux ami ! actuel : **present, of the present day, of today.**

8 How American democracy works

The United States has had the same constitution since 1787. It is the constitution of a Federation.

1. **The Federal power and the States**
   The U.S. consists of 50 federate States.
   Diplomacy, the Army and the customs administrations fall within the province of the Federal power.
   The States retain their autonomy for all matters that the law does not explicity assign to the Federal power. However the preponderance of the Federation over the States is on the increase and can be felt in many fields.

2. **The President**
   His powers are considerable indeed. He freely appoints and removes the Secretaries of State. He can govern even when the opposition has the majority in Congress.
   The President is elected for four years by popular vote. In the year preceding the presidential election, the two parties (the Democrats and the Republicans) hold primary elections and choose their candidates.
   The Vice-President, who is elected on the same "ticket", is also President of the Senate. He takes over if the President does not reach the end of his mandate because of death, resignation or impeachment.

3. **Congress**
   Congress is a bicameral assembly including the House of Representatives and the Senate.
   The number of Representatives is proportional to the number of constituents in the State. The House is the direct representation of the citizens and of their interests.
   Each State has two Senators. The Senators represent, at least theoretically, the interests of the State at federal level.

4. **The Supreme Court**
   The Supreme Court is a High Court of Justice.
   The Justices, who are nominated for life, decide whether the federal or state laws are in conformity with the Constitution. They also protect the citizens in their relations with the authorities.

THE MAKING OF AMERICA

to **work**	fonctionner	a **ci**tizen	un citoyen
		at **least**	du moins
1		theo**re**tically	en théorie
to con**sist** of	se composer de		
federate	fédéré	**4**	
the **cus**toms ad**mi**nis**tra**tion	les douanes	**Jus**tice	la Justice
		a **Jus**tice	un juge
to **fall with**in the **pro**vince of	être du ressort de	in con**for**mity with	conforme à
to as**sign** to	attribuer à		
to be **on** the in**crease**	aller en augmentant		

OTHER WORDS AND PHRASES

2

to ap**point**	nommer
to re**move** sb. (from **off**ice)	renvoyer qqn. (de son poste)
a **Se**cretary of **State**	un ministre, un secrétaire d'État
popular **vote**	le suffrage universel (1)
to **hold** an e**lec**tion	procéder à une élection
primary	primaire
the "**tic**ket" (US)	la liste des candidats d'un parti
to **take o**ver	prendre la succession
resig**na**tion	démission
im**peach**ment	suspension des pouvoirs du Président par le Congrès

3

a bi**ca**meral as**sem**bly	une assemblée à deux chambres
the **House** of Repre**sen**tatives	la Chambre des Représentants
a con**sti**tuent	un électeur

to cam**paign** for	faire campagne pour
the **plat**form of a **can**didate	le programme d'un candidat
a **show** of **hands**	un vote à mains levées
secret **bal**lot	le scrutin secret
the **bal**lot-box	l'urne
a **by**-e**lec**tion	une élection partielle
a con**sti**tuency	une circonscription
a **can**didate is re**turned**	un candidat est élu
the **Pre**sident e**lect**	le Président entre son élection (novembre) et son entrée en fonction (janvier)
the **Lame Ducks**	la période s'écoulant entre l'élection et l'entrée en fonction
the I**nau**gu**ra**tion	l'entrée en fonction du Président
the I**nau**gural Ad**dress**	le discours inaugural

---

1. Aussi : **universal suffrage**.

Grammar and exercises

Simple present and present continuous

Expression d'une vérité permanente ou d'une action habituelle → **Simple present**
— *Les Français mangent du pain, les Anglais boivent du thé.*

The French **eat** bread, the English **drink** tea.

Description s'appliquant au moment présent → **Present continuous**
— *Il est assis à table : il mange du pain mais ne boit pas de thé.*

He is sitting at the table: **he is eating** bread but **he is not drinking** tea.

Comparer :

He usually **drinks** water; why **is he drinking** wine?

Verbe ne prenant pas la forme progressive au présent :

a / les verbes de perception involontaire :

— Can you **hear** John playing the piano?
— I can't **see** anything in this fog.

b / les verbes exprimant des attitudes que l'esprit ne contrôle pas (sentiments, croyances, par exemple) ou qui n'ont pas de développement dans le temps (to want, to prefer, par exemple)

— I **want** to do this right now.
— They **believe** we are away.
— He **loves** her very deeply.
etc...

THE MAKING OF AMERICA

A *Use the correct tense (simple present or present continuous) in the following sentences:*

1 We usually (to watch) television in the evening, but tonight John (to read) and I (to knit).
2 Most young people (to wear) jeans and T-shirts. Why you (to wear) such a formal dress?
3 "Where you (to go) to?"
   "I (to go) to the hairdresser's."
4 "Where you (to spend) the summer holidays?"
   "We always (to spend) them in Italy."
5 "What you (to think) of?"
   "Of you and your stupid questions."
6 You always (to read) a lot?
7 What you (to read) right now?
8 You often (to buy) sweets for the children?
9 The President (to address) the nation every year. He now (to speak) on television.
10 I (to take) the bus to school every morning, but today my father (to drive) me.

B *Use the correct present tense in the following sentences:*

1 "Who (to knock) at the door?"
   "The milkman, I suppose."
2 What you (to want) to do tonight?
3 You (to agree) with me?
4 The prima donna who lives next door (to sing) right now. You (to hear) her?
5 I (not to understand) what you mean.
6 When he (to play) tennis, he always (to wear) white shorts. Why he (to wear) red ones today?
7 I always (to vote) for the Democratic candidate.
8 I (not to remember) what happened that day.
9 "What you (to think) of our President?"
   "I (to think) he does so little that he cannot possibly make many mistakes."
10 "What they (to do) on Saturday afternoons?"
    "They (to play) baseball or soccer."

Simple past and present perfect

Action terminée → Simple past (preterit)
— *Hier, il a lu pendant deux heures.*

   Yesterday **he read** for two hours.

— *Il a lu ce livre il y a quinze jours.*

   He read that book a fortnight ago.

Action non terminée → Present Perfect
— *Il lit depuis dix heures et demie.*

   He has been reading since 10.30.

— *Il lit depuis deux heures (= Il y a deux heures qu'il lit).*

   He has been reading for two hours.

A *Use the correct tense (simple past or present perfect) in the following sentences:*

1 His friends (to go) to the United States two years ago.
2 They (to be living) in America for two years.
3 I (not to speak) English since I left New York.
4 He (to be speaking) for a whole hour.
5 They (to go away) half-an-hour ago.

B *Make sentences as in the example:*

   Ex.: — We last saw him a month ago.
   →   — We have not seen him for a month.

1 They last wrote to us a year ago.
2 That actress acted for the last time ten years ago.
3 He was last seen a fortnight ago.
4 He last spoke to her six months ago.
5 They last made a trip to London two years ago.

C *Make sentences as in the example:*

   Ex.: — We last saw him when he came to Paris.
   → — We have not seen him since he came to Paris.

1 We last had a party for John's birthday.
2 She last called me on the phone when she was ill.
3 I last read a detective novel when I was in hospital.
4 He last gave his son a present when the child was five.
5 We last sent for the doctor when Mary had the flu.

D *Reword the sentences as in the example:*

   Ex.: — We have not seen them for two years.
   → — It is two years since we last saw them.

1 He has not shaved for three days.
2 I have not had a bite for two days.
3 Joan has not spoken German for three years.
4 He has not done any work for three months.
5 She has not written to her mother for six months.

E *Complete the following sentences using SINCE or FOR:*

1 a/ He has not shaved ... three days.
  b/ He has not shaved ... Thursday.
2 a/ She has not called me on the phone ... Monday.
  b/ She has not called me on the phone ... four days.
3 a/ The Indians have lived in reservations ... the 19th century.
  b/ The Indians have lived in reservations ... over a century.
4 a/ The United States has been independent ... two centuries.
  b/ The United States has been independent ... 1776.
5 a/ Immigration has been limited in the US ... the beginning of the 20th century.
  b/ Immigration has been limited in the US ... several decades.

Simple past and past continuous
(Prétérit et prétérit progressif)

Action ponctuelle du passé → **Simple past**
— *Le téléphone a sonné il y a une heure.*

The telephone **rang** an hour ago.

Action en cours à un moment donné du passé → **Past continuous**
— *Je dormais profondément* (action en cours) *quand le téléphone a sonné* (action ponctuelle).
I **was sleeping** soundly when the telephone **rang.**

Pluperfect and pluperfect continuous

L'action est située par rapport à un moment donné du passé :

a / Action non terminée → **Pluperfect continuous**

— *Quand la crise est arrivée, il spéculait* $\begin{cases} \textit{depuis un an.} \\ \textit{depuis l'automne 1928.} \end{cases}$

When the crisis came about, he **had been speculating**
$\begin{cases} \textbf{for} \text{ a year.} \\ \textbf{since} \text{ the autumn of 1928.} \end{cases}$

b / Action terminée → **Pluperfect**

— *Quand la crise est arrivée, il avait quitté les États-Unis depuis*
$\begin{cases} \textit{un an.} \\ \textit{l'automne 1928.} \end{cases}$

When the crisis came about, he **had been** away from the US
$\begin{cases} \textbf{for} \text{ a year.} \\ \textbf{since} \text{ the autumn of 1928.} \end{cases}$

— *Au moment où la crise est arrivée, il y avait un an qu'il avait cessé de spéculer.*

When the crisis came about, he **had given up** speculating a year **before.**

A *Use the correct past tense (simple past or past continuous) in the following sentences:*

1 She (to read) a book when John came in.
2 Mrs. Smith (to write) a letter when someone knocked at the door.
3 The pioneers'waggons were proceeding along the trail when the Indians (to attack).
4 He (to plan) to go to California when he inherited a fortune.
5 He was dreaming of further speculations when he (to hear) that he was ruined.
6 That man (to make) a fortune when the slump came about.
7 The bootlegger was selling liquor when the police (to burst) into the room.
8 I (to campaign) for that candidate when I heard that he was a crook.
9 The gold-digger (to look at) a nugget when someone attacked him.
10 We were listening to the President on television when Peter (to come in).

B *Use the correct past tense (pluperfect or pluperfect continuous) in the following sentences:*

1 He (to read) for two hours when we called on him.
2 I (not to expect) such a bad weather in Greece.
3 We did not see Peter in the States: he (to leave) three days before our arrival.
4 Because they (to have) a party the night before, they did not come with us yesterday night.
5 John (to sit) in the lobby for two hours when I arrived.
6 We (to live) in the States for ten years when Kennedy died.
7 The Congressman (to speak) for half-an-hour when he was interrupted.
8 "I (to be told) that this was the country of liberty!", said the young man, looking at a Negro slave.
9 We did not have much money then, though we (to save) for years.
10 He (to be) unhappy for years when he decided to get married.

A
Complete the following sentences using SINCE, FOR, AGO or BEFORE:

1. We have not seen the Wilsons ... a very long time.
2. As a matter of fact, we have not seen them ... Christmas.
3. When we last saw them, they had been living in the neighbourhood ... ten years.
4. They had come to our neighbourhood ten years ... .
5. How long ... did you come to live here?
6. When I called on him he had been gone ... an hour or so.
7. His secretary told me: "Mr. Smith left an hour ...".
8. It is now three hours ... that child disappeared.
9. He lost his wife two years ...; ... then he has been unable to manage his business.
10. Though he had already lived there ten years ..., he was surprised by the United States.

B
Translate into English:

1. Voyez-vous John qui joue au tennis?
2. M. et Mme Smith sont assis dans leur salon : lui est en train de lire et elle joue du piano.
3. Tous les dimanches ils vont faire une longue promenade.
4. Ils sont mariés depuis 20 ans.
5. Ils se sont mariés il y a 20 ans.
6. Quand j'ai fait la connaissance des Wilson, leur fils était mort depuis 3 mois.
7. Il était mort 3 mois auparavant dans un accident de voiture.
8. « Que faites-vous en sortant du bureau? »
   « D'habitude, je vais faire des courses, mais aujourd'hui je rentre chez moi. »
9. Il y a une heure qu'ils discutent politique.
10. Il y a une heure, John est arrivé; depuis, il joue avec mon petit garçon.
11. Ils ont habité ce quartier il y a dix ans, mais, maintenant ils vivent dans une banlieue éloignée.
12. Depuis combien de temps habitez-vous cette maison?

C Translate into English:

1 Cet Indien travaille comme laveur de carreaux depuis 2 ans.
2 Il a eu un accident il y a 3 mois.
3 Il n'avait jamais été sujet au vertige auparavant, mais depuis qu'il est tombé, il a peur de prendre des risques.
4 Depuis quelques années, des mouvements réclament l'amélioration du statut des Indiens.
5 Lorsque les Pères Pèlerins sont arrivés, il y avait des siècles que les Indiens habitaient l'Amérique.
6 Il y a 2 siècles, les Américains durent se battre pour obtenir leur indépendance.
7 Lorsque la guerre d'indépendance éclata, il y avait un certain temps que les Américains n'avaient rien à redouter de la France et de l'Espagne.
8 Quand elle est arrivée en Amérique, il y avait 3 ans que son mari y vivait.
9 Ils étaient séparés depuis 3 ans.
10 Ils ne s'étaient pas vus depuis qu'il avait quitté leur pays natal.

D Translate into English:

1 Cet homme menait une vie d'oisiveté depuis qu'il avait émigré dans un État du Sud.
2 Les troupes américaines essuyaient des revers depuis 2 ans environ lorsque Lafayette est arrivé.
3 Il y avait longtemps que Morgan était attiré par la Frontière quand il décida de partir pour l'ouest.
4 Depuis combien de temps cherchait-il de l'or quand il a trouvé sa première pépite?
5 Il y a combien de temps que la guerre de Sécession a eu lieu?
6 Il y a combien d'années qu'il a été ruiné par la crise?
7 Depuis quand les Noirs sont-ils émancipés?
8 Il était au chômage depuis 8 mois quand il a trouvé ce travail.
9 Depuis combien de temps vivez-vous de votre indemnité de chômage?
10 Il a été élu Président il y a un an; il y a un an qu'il dirige le pays.

Test

Put a cross before the right answer. Check your answers only when the test is completed.

1 The French usually ... wine and ... bread.
- ☐ a/ are drinking / eating
- ☐ b/ drink / eat
- ☐ c/ have drunk / eaten
- ☐ d/ were drinking / eating

2 "What ... on Sundays?"
"We ... tennis or golf."
- ☐ a/ do you do / play
- ☐ b/ are you doing / are playing
- ☐ c/ were you doing / were playing
- ☐ d/ did you / played

3 The day before yesterday we ... television all day.
- ☐ a/ have been watching
- ☐ b/ were watching
- ☐ c/ are watching
- ☐ d/ watched

4 We ... television ever since you ....
- ☐ a/ are watching / have left
- ☐ b/ were watching / left
- ☐ c/ watched / left
- ☐ d/ have been watching / left

5 We last ... from them five months ago.
- ☐ a/ heard
- ☐ b/ are hearing
- ☐ c/ have been hearing
- ☐ d/ had been hearing

6 He has not appeared on television ... he had an accident.
- ☐ a/ before
- ☐ b/ ago
- ☐ c/ just
- ☐ d/ since

7 Last year, he did not appear on television ... three months.
- ☐ a/ for
- ☐ b/ since
- ☐ c/ ago
- ☐ d/ just

8 People have migrated to the US ever ... its creation.
- ☐ a/ ago
- ☐ b/ since
- ☐ c/ for
- ☐ d/ before

9 It is a lot of time ... we last had a chance to sleep well.
- ☐ a/ for
- ☐ b/ before
- ☐ c/ since
- ☐ d/ just

THE MAKING OF AMERICA

10 They ... hard when I called on them.
- a/ are working
- b/ were working
- c/ have been working
- d/ been working

11 We ... some time when he phoned.
- a/ waited since
- b/ were waiting
- c/ had been waiting for
- d/ are waiting since

12 We did not meet in London for he had left the city a day ....
- a/ since
- b/ ago
- c/ before
- d/ for

13 They ... the worst for months when he died.
- a/ expect
- b/ have expected
- c/ were expecting
- d/ had been expecting

14 How long ... here, I wonder?
- a/ do you sit
- b/ are you sitting
- c/ have you been sitting
- d/ you sat

15 The battle of Wounded Knee took place nearly ...
- a/ for a century
- b/ since a century
- c/ a century ago
- d/ a century before

16 The Americans ... Independance Day on the 4th of July.
- a/ celebrate
- b/ are celebrating
- c/ are used to celebrate
- d/ use to celebrate

17 ... ago did the rebellion take place?
- a/ How much
- b/ When
- c/ How many
- d/ How long

18 In the 19th century, industrial towns ... in the new regions.
- a/ appearing
- b/ was appearing
- c/ appeared
- d/ have appeared

19 The conflict had been latent for years when Lincoln ... elected.
- a/ has been
- b/ was
- c/ had been
- d/ would be

20 When the war ended, he had been fighting ... 4 years.
- a/ for
- b/ since
- c/ in
- d/ while

1 New England

New England, which was settled as early as the beginning of the 17th century, includes the six north-eastern states of the U.S. In many ways it resembles old England.

1 An agricultural region

In spite of the efforts made to enlarge the farms in order to mechanize production, there are still a lot of small farms in New England. In many of its agricultural pursuits, New England therefore faces competition from other areas.

Dairying is the leading agricultural resource. Whereas in some areas it is a specialized industry, in many others, it is part of general farming or is associated with poultry-raising.

Some farmers have specialized in the cultivation of potatoes (Maine), cranberries (used to make the cranberry sauce which traditionally accompanies turkey on Thanksgiving Day), apples, pears, peaches, red-currants or tobacco.

New England supplies the big conurbations of the East coast with fresh milk, quality eggs and fresh fruit.

2 Changing industrial patterns

The lack of coal, oil or other resources has entailed an inevitable decline in the traditional industries: textiles, timber, and leather.

But the development of new industries: electronics and metal-using industries, is bolstered by the federal authorities. Sixty per cent of the workers in the electronics industry live in the Boston area.

3 Boston

It is the main city in that area, with a low percentage of Black inhabitants.

The Americans regard Boston as an aristocratic city.

It boasts two famous universities: Harvard and the M.I.T. (Massachussets Institute of Technology).

But it is also a major banking centre, an important port (though it has never been able to compete with New York), and an industrial city in full development (science-based industries, machine-tools, defence-based industries, electronics, etc...).

THE MAIN REGIONS OF THE UNITED STATES

settled	colonisé(e)
to in**clude**	comprendre
to re**sem**ble	ressembler à

1

there are **still**	il y a encore
a pur**suit**	une entreprise
therefore	donc
to **face**	se trouver en face de
dairying	l'industrie laitière
leading	principal(e)
where**as**	alors que
poultry-raising	l'élevage des volailles
cranberries	airelles (cousinettes)
a **tur**key	une dinde
Thanksgiving Day (1)	le jour d'actions de grâces
red-currants	groseilles
a **co**nur**ba**tion	une conurbation (2)

2

patterns	structures
lack	manque
oil	pétrole
to en**tail**	entraîner
timber	bois
leather	cuir
bolstered	soutenu, encouragé

3

per**cen**tage	pourcentage
to re**gard**	considérer
to **boast**	1/ se vanter 2/ posséder
ma**chine**-tools	machines-outils
de**fence**-based **in**dustries	industries de l'armement

OTHER WORDS AND PHRASES

the **cradle** of A**mer**ican **Pu**ritanism	le berceau du Puritanisme américain
a **farm**stead	une ferme et ses dépendances
agri**cul**tural **im**plements	outils agricoles
the **dai**ry	la laiterie
dairy pro**duce**	les produits laitiers
a **milk can**	un bidon de lait
the **fowls**	les volailles
the **hen**-roost	le poulailler
a **hen**	une poule
a **goose** (3)	une oie
the **tur**key-cock	le dindon
the **Gui**nea-fowl	la pintade
to **lay eggs**	pondre des œufs
a **new**-laid **egg**	un œuf frais pondu

---

1. Fête célébrée aux États-Unis le dernier jeudi de novembre. Elle commémore l'arrivée en Amérique d'un bateau venu d'Angleterre un an après celui des Pères Pèlerins.
2. Conurbation = agglomération d'unités urbaines.
3. Pluriel : **geese**.

2 New York and the Megalopolis

Along the east coast of the U.S., a huge urban area stretches over 700 miles. To the north it merges into New England. It includes such cities as New York, Philadelphia, and Washington. It has been called the Megalopolis.

1 The brain of the United States
In this area there live over 40 million inhabitants who earn one-third of the incomes and salaries earned by American citizens.
The area produces over 25 % of the total American industrial production.
Here the best-known universities are to be found: Columbia, Princeton, Yale, and Harvard.

2 New York
Wall Street and the huge office skyscrapers, the biggest hotels, the Broadway theatres, the museums, the largest stores, Central Park, Harlem, the docks, the slums, money, luxury and poverty are concentrated on Manhattan Island.
But there are only two million residents in Manhattan.
Factories, airports and some residential districts are located on Long Island.
The port of New York ranks second in the world.
NYC is an industrial as well as a business giant: clothing, publishing and printing, chemical and foodstuff industries.

3 Washington
The federal capital is an administrative centre. It is the seat of the federal government, of Congress and of the foreign embassies.
Town-planners and architects took great pains so that this artificial city, built in the late 18th century, should enjoy open spaces and broad avenues.
Over half the population is black (perhaps because servants are in great demand).

4 The other cities of the Megalopolis
Philadelphia is a huge industrial conurbation with a very important port.
The suburbs of Baltimore, whose activity is based mainly on iron and copper, merge into those of Washington.

THE MAIN REGIONS OF THE UNITED STATES

huge	immense
stretches **o**ver	s'étend sur
to **merge** into	se fondre avec

1

the **brain**	le cerveau
over 40 **mil**lion	plus de 40 millions de
to **earn**	gagner
one-third	un tiers
an **in**come	un revenu

2

a **thea**tre	un théâtre ou un cinéma
a **store**	un grand magasin
a **slum**	un quartier de taudis
luxury	le luxe
poverty	la pauvreté
a **fac**tory	une usine
to be lo**ca**ted	être situé
ranks second	vient au second rang
NYC	New York City
the **clo**thing **in**dustry	(l'industrie de) la confection
the **pub**lishing **in**dustry	l'édition
the **print**ing **in**dustry	l'imprimerie
foodstuff **in**dustries	les industries de produits alimentaires

3

the **seat**	le siège
an **em**bassy	une ambassade
a **town**-planner	un(e) urbaniste
to **take great pains**	mettre tous ses soins
in the **late** 18th **cen**tury	vers la fin du XVIIIᵉ siècle
open **spa**ces	espaces verts
broad	large
to **be** in **great de**mand	être très recherché

4

the **su**burbs	la banlieue
mainly	essentiellement
iron	le fer
copper	le cuivre

OTHER WORDS AND PHRASES

---

the me**tro**polis	la capitale
a **dis**trict	un quartier
a **block**	un pâté d'immeubles
a pe**des**trian	un piéton
a **traf**fic jam	un embouteillage
the **Sub**way (1)	le métro
a de**part**ment-store	un grand magasin
a **chain**-store	un magasin à succursales

---

1. GB : **the tube**.

3 The Middle West

In the heart of the U.S. stretch vast plains particularly fertile and therefore quite suitable for corn-growing and cattle-breeding.

1 The Corn Belt

Corn is the American cereal: in the past, it was grown by the Indians, and the Europeans discovered it when they arrived on this new continent.

The Corn Belt accounts for half of the U.S. crop, itself equivalent to half the world total.

Rotation crops include soya beans, wheat, oats and alfalfa. The corn produced is used for human consumption (breakfast cereals, corn on the cob), but its main use is in the feeding of livestock (pigs, poultry). Oxen are also fattened on corn, and sheep feed on the grass growing on the corn fields.

The meat-packing stations, or slaughterhouses, are located in Chicago, Kansas City and Saint-Louis.

2 The Wheat Belt

Wheat is grown mainly in North and South Dakota (spring wheat) and in Kansas (winter wheat).

The farmsteads are huge, production has been entirely mechanized. However the yield is often low and the farmers often derive more income from the sale of cattle than from the sale of wheat.

3 The Great Lakes

To the north of the High Plains, along the Canadian border, the Great Lakes form a sort of inland sea. Canals connect them with the main waterways of the North-East and with the Mississippi.

Ships which carry coal, timber and ore sail across the Lakes. Chicago is the main urban centre of this area. It is a major reception and distribution depot for grain, the first centre for the meat-packing trade. Steel-works are located on the shores of Lake Michigan, and oil is refined in Chicago and distributed from there.

The Middle West is the nation's leading producer of automobiles with the two cities of Detroit (Ford, General Motors, Chrysler, etc...) and Cleveland (Ford, etc...).

THE MAIN REGIONS OF THE UNITED STATES

in the **heart** of	au cœur de
suitable for	adapté à
cattle-breeding	élevage

1

corn (1)	maïs
the **Corn Belt**	la région où l'on cultive le maïs
to ac**count** for	avoir à son actif
crop	récolte
ro**ta**tion **crops**	les cultures qui entrent en assolement avec le maïs
soya beans	le soja
wheat	le blé
oats	l'avoine
al**fal**fa (2)	la luzerne (US)
corn on the **cob**	épi de maïs que l'on mange grillé ou bouilli
livestock	bétail
oxen (3)	les bovins
fattened	engraissé(s)
to **feed** on	se nourrir de
a **meat**-packing **sta**tion = a **slaugh**terhouse	un abattoir

2

the **yield**	la production
low	peu important
to de**rive** sth. from	tirer qch. de

3

border	frontière
an **inland sea**	une mer intérieure
to con**nect**	relier
a **wa**terway	une voie navigable
coal	charbon
timber	bois
ore	minerai
a **steel**-works	une aciérie
the **shore**	la rive (lac ou mer)
oil	le pétrole

OTHER WORDS AND PHRASES

---

raw materials	les matières premières
finished **pro**ducts	les produits finis
a **car** factory	une usine d'automobiles
the as**sem**bly line	la chaîne de montage
as**sem**bly line pro**duc**tion = **mov**ing-band pro**duc**tion	le travail à la chaîne
to **work** on the as**sem**bly line	travailler à la chaîne
the **fore**man	le contremaître
labour = **man**power	la main-d'œuvre
mass pro**duc**tion	la fabrication en série
shoddy **goods**	marchandises de mauvaise qualité

---

1. GB : maïs = **maize, Indian corn.**
2. GB : **lucern.**
3. Singulier : **an ox.**

4 The Mississippi

In the Indian tongue, "Mississippi" <u>means</u> "Big River", and the Mississippi River certainly <u>deserves</u> this name. With its two <u>tributaries,</u> the Missouri and the Ohio, the Mississippi <u>drains</u> a huge basin. It receives water from 31 American states and 2 Canadian provinces.

1 The Mississippi in the olden days

The Mississippi River was first explored by a Frenchman, Cavelier de La Salle, in the 17th century.

In the course of the 18th century the river became an important waterway on which were transported cereals, timber, and cotton.

For a long time, the Mississippi river marked <u>the boundary</u> between civilized and unexplored territories. Colonization did not go further west before the beginning of the 19th century.

In the 19th century the Mississippi became the most important waterway in the U.S.. The <u>paddle-wheel steamboats</u> which sailed up and down the river, carrying cotton, sugar cane, or passengers, have become part of the American mythology thanks to Mark Twain but also thanks to the cinema.

After the Civil War, however, the importance of the Mississippi <u>decreased</u> <u>slightly</u> until the opening of the Panama Canal.

2 The Mississippi today

Improvements in the river and in available means of conveyance <u>account for</u> the <u>increase</u> in traffic on the Mississippi.

<u>As a barge</u> can carry <u>as much as</u> one million <u>gallons</u> of oil at rates lower than <u>railroad</u> rates, there is a heavy traffic of <u>freighters</u> on the Mississippi.

<u>Besides,</u> manufacturing industries have been attracted to the Mississippi river sites by the facilities offered.

Specialized barges and <u>towboats</u> have been developed for the transportation of some <u>commodities.</u> Coal, steel, grain, automobiles, sugar and oil are the main commodities carried by <u>river freight.</u>

But there are still excursion steamers on the Mississippi; they have, <u>to some extent,</u> <u>preserved</u> the tradition of the 19th century <u>showboats.</u>

THE MAIN REGIONS OF THE UNITED STATES

to **mean**	signifier
to de**serve**	mériter
a **tribut**ary	un affluent
to **drain**	drainer

1

in the **old**en days	autrefois
the **bound**ary	la limite
a **paddle-wheel steam**boat	un bateau à roues
to de**crease**	diminuer
slightly	quelque peu

2

to ac**count** for	expliquer, être responsable de
an **in**crease	une augmentation
a **barge**	une péniche
as **much** as	jusqu'à
a **gall**on	un gallon (1)
rate	cours, prix
railroad	chemin de fer
a **freight**er = a **cargo**	un cargo
be**sides**	de plus
a **tow**boat	un remorqueur
a com**mo**dity	une marchandise
river freight	transport fluvial
to some ex**tent**	dans une certaine mesure
to pre**serve**	conserver
a **show**boat (2)	un bateau spectacle

OTHER WORDS AND PHRASES

"the **swim**ming vol**ca**no" (3)	le volcan qui nage
a **gam**bler	un joueur (de salle de jeux)
a **rous**tabout	U.S. : un débardeur
a **pack**ët(-boat)	un bateau de passagers (4)
a **lin**er	un paquebot (5)
the **car**go	la cargaison
to (**un**)**load**	(dé)charger
to **sail down stream**	naviguer avec le courant
to **sail up stream**	naviguer à contre-courant
a **wharf**	un quai (de port)

---

1. Soit 4,54 litres en Grande-Bretagne, et 3,78 litres aux États-Unis.
2. Terme réservé aux bateaux à roues qui naviguaient sur le Mississippi et offraient spectacles et salles de jeux. Appelés aussi "**palaces on wheels**".
3. Surnom donné aux bateaux à roues du Mississippi.
4. A donné le mot français : « paquebot ».
5. Ne pas oublier que l'on emploie le pronom féminin (**she**) pour parler d'un bateau en anglais.

5 California

California, which was originally colonized by the Spaniards, has been part of the U.S. since 1848. As early as 1849, the Gold Rush led to a stupendous development.
Today California is the most go-ahead state in the U.S.

1 Agriculture
An exceptionally mild climate has made possible the cultivation of fruit (oranges, peaches, apricots, grapes). Some of the farmsteads are villages where fruit is processed as well as grown.
Vineyards are to be seen almost everywhere, and California produces wines whose quality is improving steadily.
The number of agricultural workers is higher than in any other state. In addition, Mexican farm-hands are employed seasonally.
The livestock industry (more concerned with sheep than oxen) also holds an important place.

2 Industry
The drilling of oil since 1860 has permitted the development of powerful industries which also use natural gas and the electricity produced by the generating-stations of the Sierra Nevada.
Whereas the shipyards have experienced a decline in their activity, the aircraft and automobile industries are thriving.
The foodstuff industries (processing and canning of fruit and fish in particular) are extremely important.
In addition to all this, California is the world's leading centre for the motion picture industry. Hollywood is a suburb of Los Angeles.

3 San Francisco and Los Angeles (Frisco and L. A.)
San Francisco is not merely a picturesque city, famous for its hippy communities. It is also a big industrial centre and a major sea-port on the West coast.
However, the development of its activities is checked by the lack of room for expansion.
On the contrary, L. A., which stretches out over 60 miles, ranks second among American cities. With its ever-developing industrial activities, it is the real capital of the West.

originally	tout d'abord
the **Spa**niards	les Espagnols
the **Gold Rush**	la Ruée vers l'Or
stu**pen**dous	prodigieux
go-ahead	actif

1

a **mild cli**mate	un climat tempéré
grapes	raisins
processed	traité
a **vine**yard	une vigne (1)
in ad**di**tion	de plus
a **farm**-hand = an agri**cul**tural **work**er	un ouvrier agricole
seasonally	de façon saisonnière
livestock	bétail
sheep	les moutons

2

to **drill oil**	faire des forages
a **ge**nerating-**sta**tion = a **pow**er-**plant**	une centrale électrique
where**as**	alors que
a **ship**yard	un chantier naval
the **air**craft **in**dustry	les constructions aéronautiques
thriving	prospère(s)
to **can fruit**	mettre des fruits en conserves

3

merely	simplement
to **check**	enrayer
lack of **room**	manque d'espace
to **rank se**cond	venir au second rang

OTHER WORDS AND PHRASES

ripe fruit	fruit(s) mûr(s)
to **pick fruit**	cueillir des fruits
a **lad**der	une échelle
to **bend down**	se courber
spoilt fruit	fruits gâtés, abîmés
rotten	pourri
pre**serves**	conserves
jam	confiture
marmalade	confiture d'oranges
a **green**grocer	un marchand de fruits et légumes

---

1. **Vine** : de la vigne

6 Texas

Texas is popularly known as the "Lone Star State" because of the single star in its flag.

The dynamism of its economy marks Texas out among the states of the South.

1 Traditional Texas

In the 19th century, cattle-breeding was the main economic activity of Texas. The cow-boys were in charge of the huge herds of cattle which belonged to the ranchers.

The cow-boy, with his stetson hat, his high-heeled boots and his leather leggings, has become the picturesque hero of many a western.

In spite of the rapid development of oil and industry, the tradition of cattle-breeding endures.

With more than 10 million head of cattle and over 5 million sheep, Texas still ranks first for cattle-breeding. The herds remain mainly in the coastal region, the eastern part of Texas being devoted to the cultivation of cotton.

2 Mineral resources

The subsoil is extremely rich in mineral resources which are Texas's fortune.

Texas produces more sulphur and salt than any other region of the U.S.. As to oil, which was first drilled for in 1901, it represents 45 % of the total American production. The refineries of Houston and Galveston process this oil which is afterwards exported.

3 Industry

These energy sources have made possible the setting up of plants which process ores imported from Latin America.

In Houston there are numerous huge steel-works; Mobile has specialized in aluminum, Corpus Christi in zinc, Texas City in tin.

The main city is Houston, which is both an industrial centre and a port. It is also the largest cotton-market in the world.

THE MAIN REGIONS OF THE UNITED STATES

a **fla**g	un drapeau
to **mark** out	distinguer

1

a **herd**	un troupeau
to be**long** to	appartenir à
high-heeled	à talons hauts
leggings (1)	jambières
to en**dure** (2)	durer
coastal	côtière
de**vo**ted to	consacré(e) à

2

the **sub**soil	le sous-sol
sulphur	soufre
as to	quant à
a re**fi**nery	une raffinerie
afterwards	par la suite

3

the **set**ting **up**	l'installation
a **plant** (3)	une usine
ores	minerais
a **steel**-works	une aciérie
aluminum (4)	l'aluminium
tin	l'étain
both	à la fois

OTHER WORDS AND PHRASES

a **horse**-rider	un cavalier
to **ride** a **horse**	monter à cheval
a **sad**dle	une selle
the **spurs**	les éperons
to **spur** a **horse**	éperonner un cheval
to **spur** **some**body on	stimuler quelqu'un
to **drive** a **herd**	conduire un troupeau
a **drove**	un troupeau (de bœufs) en marche
a co**rral**	un enclos à bestiaux
a **long**horn	un bœuf à longues cornes (Texas)
US **oil** = GB pe**tro**leum	le pétrole
crude (oil)	(pétrole) brut
shale oil	huile de schistes bitumineux
a **fuel**	un combustible
an **oil**-field	un gisement de pétrole
an **oil**-deposit	une poche de pétrole
drilling	le forage
a **drill**-hole	un forage
a **pipe**-line	un oléoduc
a **tank**er	un pétrolier

---

1. Aussi appelées "**chaps**", abréviation de "**chaparejos**".
2. Faux-ami ! **To endure** ne veut que très rarement dire « endurer » (**to bear**).
3. G.B. : **a factory, a works**.
4. Attention à l'orthographe et à l'accentuation ! U.S. **aluminum** = G.B. **aluminium**.

7 The South

The South seems more closely bound up with its past than any other region of the United States. However, over the past few decades, the rise of industry in the South has been an outstanding fact.

1 The past
Before the arrival of the first settlers, the Indians cultivated corn and tobacco. The colonists grew the same crops, to which rice and indigo were added later.
To cope with the shortage of servants, they employed indentured labour. But the Negro slaves, imported from Africa as "ebony wood" and sold in auction-sales, soon became the backbone of farming.
Cotton was king and the economy was based on a one-crop system, which implied many drawbacks: exhaustion of the land, the ravages of insects, and dependence on imports (foodstuffs and manufactured goods) and on climatic conditions.

2 The diversification of agriculture
Nowadays only one tenth of the Cotton Belt is under cotton, but efficiency of production has been achieved.
Tobacco is still the leading crop in a few regions, but other agricultural productions have been developed: cattle-breeding, poultry-raising, dairying, and citrus and sugar-cane crops.

3 Industry
Industrial development has made rapid strides with the building of hydro-electric plants.
At the same time, the exploitation of oil and other mineral resources has entailed the development of new industries (the chemical industry) and improvements in the traditional industries (textiles, timber, paper, and steel).

4 Urban concentrations
The industrial development, added to a thriving tourist industry, has resulted in a wave of urban concentrations. New Orleans, Houston, Memphis, and Dallas have experienced phenomenal growth.
The South, however, remains relatively poor, with social, economic and racial problems. The Blacks sometimes outnumber the Whites. The conflict, though not always violent, is, nevertheless, latent and enduring.

THE MAIN REGIONS OF THE UNITED STATES

closely	étroitement
bound up with	lié à
a decade	une décennie
outstanding	marquant

1

to cope with	(pour) pallier
shortage	pénurie
indentured labour (1)	les « engagés »
"ebony wood"	le « bois d'ébène »
an auction-sale	une vente aux enchères
the backbone	1 / la colonne vertébrale 2 / l'armature
one-crop system	monoculture
to imply	impliquer
a drawback	un inconvénient
exhaustion	épuisement

2

(fields) under cotton	mis en coton
to achieve	réussir
citrus fruit (2)	les agrumes
sugar-cane	la canne à sucre

3

to make strides	faire des progrès
to entail	entraîner

4

thriving	florissant(e)
to result in	entraîner
a wave	une vague
to outnumber	être plus nombreux que
nevertheless	néanmoins
enduring	durable

OTHER WORDS AND PHRASES

raw cotton	le coton brut
to pick cotton	cueillir le coton
a bale	une balle (de coton)
to spin, spun, spun	filer (la laine, le coton)
a spinning-frame	un métier à filer
a cotton-mill	une filature de coton
to weave, wove, woven	tisser
a hand-loom	un métier à tisser à la main
a power-loom	un métier mécanique

---

1. Les « engagés » étaient des immigrants européens qui n'avaient pas les moyens de payer la traversée. En échange de leur passage, de la nourriture et du logement, ils s'engageaient à servir un maître pendant un certain nombre d'années; après quoi, ils étaient libres.
2. Un citron : a lemon.

Grammar and exercises

Sequence of tenses
(Concordance des temps)

A. FUTUR

Proposition principale au futur → **Subordonnée au présent**
après une conjonction de temps, « if » ou « suppose » :
— *Je partirai dès qu'il s'arrêtera de pleuvoir.*

I'll go as soon as it stops raining.

— *Je partirai si vous le voulez.*

I'll go if you want me to.

B. CONDITIONNEL

a / Proposition principale au conditionnel présent
→ **Subordonnée au prétérit** :
— *Je serais ravie si vous veniez de bonne heure.*

I'd be delighted if you came early.

— *S'il était ici, il vous aiderait*

If he were here he'd help you.

Noter que, pour le verbe « to be », la forme est « were » pour toutes les personnes (forme du prétérit modal).

b / Proposition principale au conditionnel passé
→ **Subordonnée au « pluperfect »** (had + participe passé)
— *S'il avait été ici, il vous aurait aidé.*
If he had been here, he'd have helped you.

THE MAIN REGIONS OF THE UNITED STATES

A *Use the correct tense of the verb in brackets in the following sentences:*

1 We'll enlarge our farm if we (to find) the money necessary.
2 That farmer will be faced with difficulties if he (not to improve) his equipment.
3 When you (to decide) to go, we'll take you to the station.
4 The family will have dinner the moment the father (to get) home.
5 That Mexican will get a job on a farm if he (can).
6 When you (to feel) like taking a holiday, we'll go to California.
7 As soon as he (to get) his High School Diploma, he'll apply to enter College.
8 If you (to feel) like living in NYC, I won't stop you.
9 I hope you'll let me know when they (to come).
10 If the crop (to be) too poor next summer, we'll have to import wheat.

B *Use the correct tense of the verb in brackets:*

1 They'd grow oranges if the climate (to be) mild enough.
2 We'd live in Boston if we (can) afford it.
3 Supposing we (to have) to live in the country, where would you like to go?
4 Provided I (to be) offered a good job, I wouldn't mind moving to another state.
5 If they (to work) in NYC, they'd probably buy a house in Long Island.
6 If rents (to be) not so high in Manhattan, we'd live there.
7 We would have turned to another activity if we (to find) it advantageous.
8 I wouldn't have bought such shoddy goods if I (to know).
9 If we (to have) time, we would have taken a trip on a Mississippi steamer.
10 If I (not to read) books by Mark Twain, I wouldn't have been able to imagine what life on the Mississippi was like in the past.

Reported speech
(Style indirect)

Accord des subordonnées dépendant de :
"He said that...", "He told me that...", etc.

a / Principale au présent ou au « present perfect »
→ **Subordonnée au temps du style direct :**
— He has said to me: "I'll be with you tomorrow."
→ He has said to me (that) he'll be with us tomorrow.
— He keeps telling me: "You're a fool."
→ He keeps telling me (that) I'm a fool.

b / Principale au prétérit
→ **1 / les paroles prononcées au présent sont rapportées au prétérit :**

— "I'm reading a good book", he said.
→ He said (that) he was reading a good book.

2 / les paroles prononcées au futur sont rapportées au conditionnel :

— "I'll play tennis with you tomorrow", he said.
→ He said (that) he would play tennis with me the following day.

3 / les paroles prononcées au prétérit ou au « present perfect » sont rapportées au « pluperfect » :

— In his letter he said: "I've been very ill for the past few days."
→ He wrote (that) he had been very ill for the past few days.

4 / les paroles prononcées au conditionnel sont rapportées au même temps :

— "I'd like to spend the holidays with you if I could", he said.
→ He said (that) he'd like to spend the holidays with us if he could.

THE MAIN REGIONS OF THE UNITED STATES

A *Turn the following sentences into reported speech:*

1 He writes in his letter: "I'll try to get a job in the canning factory."
2 The Wilsons keep saying: "We'd like to go to California if we could afford the trip."
3 As he is picking cotton, he keeps thinking: "How I'd like to be the plantation owner!"
4 She never stops saying: "If I went to Hollywood, I'd become a star in no time at all."
5 I usually tell her: "You'd better give up your daydreaming and work harder here."

B *Turn into reported speech:*

1 She wrote in her letter: "We are doing very well and earning a lot of money this year."
2 They told me: "We've made such a lot of money from the sale of our cattle that we can hardly believe it."
3 She said: "I'll come if I must."
4 My brother wrote to me: "We would like to go to the West coast next summer."
5 Mrs Smith said to me: "My little boy has just told me: 'I'd like to be a cowboy'."
6 The teacher said: "The mineral resources of Texas have made possible the setting up of plants."
7 Peter Wilson wrote to me: "I now have a very good job at the chemical plant."
8 The boss told me: "We're going to build the largest tanker ever built."
9 The teacher said: "Cotton is the leading crop in the South."
10 Mary writes in her letter: "I have bought beautiful hand-woven materials."
11 Mr Pendleton told me: "If you don't mind moving to another region, we can send you to Houston."
12 He added: "We're opening a new branch there."

Reported speech: questions

Les paroles prononcées sont des questions → **Subordonnée introduite par un terme interrogatif.**
On respecte la règle de la concordance des temps.

— "Will you come to the party?" he asked.
→ He asked me whether I would come to the party.
— "What's the matter with you?" he asked.
→ He asked me what the matter was (with me).
— "How did you do it?" he asked.
→ He asked me how I had done it.

Reported speech: orders

Les paroles prononcées sont des ordres donnés à l'aide des verbes : to order, to demand, to ask, to say, to tell, etc...

→ **1°/ Verbe + complément + subordonnée infinitive :**
— He told me: "Put the book on the table."
→ He told me to put the book on the table.

2°/ Verbe + that + subordonnée au subjonctif :
— He ordered that the prisoner (should) be set free.

Had better, would { rather / sooner }

Ces expressions sont toujours suivies de **l'infinitif incomplet** :

— *Je ferais mieux de travailler (plutôt que de jouer).*
  I'd better work rather than play.

— *J'aimerais mieux jouer que travailler.*
  I'd { rather / sooner } play than work.

THE MAIN REGIONS OF THE UNITED STATES

A *Turn into reported speech:*

1 He asked us: "When will you go to Florida?"
2 The teacher asked: "Who is going to answer that question?"
3 She asked us: "Where did you spend your holidays?"
4 He asked me: "Why have you said that to Mary?"
5 They asked us: "Would you care to come to our party?"
6 She asked: "What will happen if we don't go?"
7 John asked you: "Whose book is this?"
8 The child asked: "Which way should I go?"
9 Mary asked: "How can you say that to a child?"
10 I asked her: "When will you be coming then?"

B *Turn into reported speech:*

1 He said to her: "Come here at once!"
2 She told him: "Don't speak to me like that!"
3 The gangster ordered: "Give me the money at once or I'll kill you all!"
4 The judge said: "Bring in the defendant!"
5 My mother told me: "Don't bite your nails!"

C *Using HAD BETTER (= 'D BETTER), make sentences with the expressions in brackets:*

1 I'd like to go to the cinema but (work for my exam).
2 John plays American football but (play a less brutal game).
3 The kidnappers told him that he (pay the ransom) if he didn't want his son to be killed.
4 You (read a good book) instead of that rubbishy detective novel.
5 Instead of going to the cinema I (stay at home): the film is said to be very poor.

Defective verbs

CAN exprime la **capacité physique ou intellectuelle**, la **vraisemblance**, quelquefois la permission.
Équivalent : **to be able to.**

MAY exprime l'**éventualité** et la **permission**.
Équivalents : a / constructions avec **« perhaps »** (éventualité).
b / **to be allowed to** (permission).

MUST exprime l'**obligation** et la **forte probabilité**.
Équivalents : a / **to have to** (obligation)
b / constructions avec **« certainly »**, **« to be sure to »**.

Ces défectifs sont tous suivis de l'**infinitif incomplet**; ils ne prennent pas « s » à la 3ᵉ personne du singulier.

OUGHT TO & **SHOULD** + infinitif incomplet :

a / **Conseil** : — You { **ought to** / **should** } read this book.

Vous devriez lire ce livre.

b / **Probabilité** : — This book is by James: it { **ought to** / **should** } be good.

Ce livre est de James : il devrait être bon.

Noter que, à la forme négative, **« shouldn't »** est beaucoup plus fréquent que **« oughtn't to »**.

NEED & **DARE** peuvent également se construire comme des verbes ordinaires. A la forme négative, noter la différence entre :

a / I didn't **need** to go to their party, so I stayed at home.

b / I **needn't** have gone to their party: nobody would have noticed my absence.

Dans le deuxième cas, on a accompli une action qui n'était pas indispensable.

THE MAIN REGIONS OF THE UNITED STATES

A *Turn into the simple past:*

1 The children may not watch television tonight.
2 You may not apply for a government loan.
3 Our son may not enter Harvard.
4 I may not go to the theatre.
5 Pedestrians may not cross the streets when traffic-lights are green.

B *Reconstruct the following sentences using a/ SHOULD, b/ OUGHT TO, as in the example:*

Ex.: — Why don't you get up earlier?
→   a/ You should get up earlier.
    b/ You ought to get up earlier.

1 Why doesn't she dress better?
2 Why isn't he less rude?
3 Why don't they go to Florida?
4 Why doesn't he work better?
5 Why don't they raise his salary?
6 Why didn't he tell the truth?
7 Why weren't they more understanding?
8 Why didn't they develop the region earlier?

C *Complete the following sentences, using DIDN'T NEED TO or NEEDN'T HAVE, according to the meaning of the sentence:*

1 You (to speak) so rudely to her; why did you do so?
2 I (to save) money, so I spent it all and enjoyed myself.
3 I (to save) so much money: I don't know what to do with it.
4 She (to spend) so much time at the university since she has forgotten everything she learnt.
5 We (to take) the trip, so we stayed at home.
6 They (to have) taken such drastic measures: now they have to undo what they did.

D *Translate into English:*

1 Il agrandira sa ferme quand il aura obtenu un prêt.
2 Notre fille s'installera à la campagne dès qu'elle le pourra.
3 Quand ces porcs seront assez gras, nous les vendrons.
4 S'ils n'avaient pas mécanisé leur travail, les fermiers du Middle West obtiendraient un rendement plus bas.
5 S'il ne travaillait pas à la chaîne, cet ouvrier d'usine serait moins malheureux.
6 Si la qualité des vins de Californie ne s'était pas améliorée, ils ne pourraient rivaliser avec les vins français.

E *Translate into English:*

1 Il dit qu'il s'installera à San Francisco.
2 Il ne cesse de dire qu'il voudrait bien avoir une belle situation, mais il ne travaille pas.
3 Elle dit que, si ses parents avaient été plus riches, elle aurait pu faire ses études à Harvard.
4 Il m'a écrit que la récolte serait bonne cette année.
5 Ils avaient dit qu'ils ne resteraient pas longtemps ici.
6 Il m'a expliqué que le manque d'espace gênait San Francisco dans son expansion.
7 Cette ravissante jeune personne m'a dit qu'elle aimerait beaucoup aller à Hollywood.
8 J'ai demandé à ce Texan comment il avait fait fortune.
9 Je leur ai demandé à qui était ce ranch.
10 Ils m'ont demandé si j'aimerais aller au cinéma voir un western.

F *Translate into English:*

1 Ses parents lui ont dit de se taire.
2 Le shérif a ordonné aux voleurs de se rendre.
3 Puis il a donné l'ordre qu'on les pende.
4 L'ingénieur a ordonné qu'on fasse un nouveau forage.
5 Il a demandé au chauffeur de s'arrêter à une station-service.

THE MAIN REGIONS OF THE UNITED STATES

G *Translate into English:*

1 Vous feriez mieux de construire des appartements plutôt que des immeubles de bureaux.
2 Nous aimerions mieux habiter dans une banlieue résidentielle que dans le centre de Manhattan.
3 Vous feriez mieux d'élever du bétail plutôt que de perdre votre temps à cultiver le blé.
4 Ils auraient mieux fait de ne pas vous écouter.
5 J'aurais mieux aimé descendre le Mississippi plutôt que de le remonter : cela aurait été plus facile.

H *Translate into English:*

1 Ils ne pourront pas venir demain.
2 Il se peut qu'ils soient en retard.
3 Puis-je vous emprunter ce livre ?
4 Nous pourrions peut-être aller sur la côte est pendant les vacances ?
5 Il ne faut pas que la ville prenne trop d'expansion.
6 Ils ont sûrement pris leur voiture : elle n'est pas dans leur garage.
7 Ils nous ont dit que nous devrions bien essayer d'améliorer notre production.
8 C'est Mr Burns qui nous a dit cela : ce devrait être un bon conseil.

I *Translate into English:*

1 Il n'était pas nécessaire qu'il vienne : il est donc resté à San Francisco.
2 Ce n'était vraiment pas la peine que je leur téléphone : ils ne m'ont pas écoutée.
3 Ce n'était pas la peine que vous nous expliquiez la situation : nous l'avions fort bien comprise.
4 Il n'était pas indispensable que je parle : je n'ai donc rien dit.

GRAMMAR AND EXERCISES

Test

1 They'll come as soon as they ... .
- □ a/ can
- □ b/ could
- □ c/ would
- □ d/ will be able to

2 When the crisis ... over I'll get a job.
- □ a/ be
- □ b/ is
- □ c/ were
- □ d/ will be

3 I'll talk to him whenever you ... it's necessary.
- □ a/ thought
- □ b/ have thought
- □ c/ think
- □ d/ will have thought

4 We'd like this country if the climate ... milder.
- □ a/ has been
- □ b/ is
- □ c/ would be
- □ d/ were

5 If I ... here he wouldn't have talked to you like that.
- □ a/ have been
- □ b/ were
- □ c/ had been
- □ d/ would have been

6 If you worked harder you ... better.
- □ a/ will succeed
- □ b/ would succeed
- □ c/ succeeded
- □ d/ had succeeded

7 He keeps complaining that ... a failure.
- □ a/ he is
- □ b/ he were
- □ c/ he be
- □ d/ he would be

8 If ... a failure he wouldn't earn so much money.
- □ a/ he be
- □ b/ he were
- □ c/ he is
- □ d/ he would be

9 He said he ... to California the year ... .
- □ a/ had been / ago
- □ b/ had been / before
- □ c/ has been / before
- □ d/ would go / ago

10 He told us that he would have liked to come with us if ... .
- □ a/ he can
- □ b/ he were able to
- □ c/ he had been able to
- □ d/ he could

THE MAIN REGIONS OF THE UNITED STATES

11 The farmers asked us ... such a crop.
- a/ how we had obtained
- b/ how had we obtained
- c/ how obtain
- d/ how would we obtain

12 He ordered that the milk ... at that price.
- a/ should be sold
- b/ is sold
- c/ will be sold
- d/ would be sold

13 I'd rather ... a little longer but I must ... .
- a/ to stay / to go
- b/ stay / go
- c/ stayed / went
- d/ will have stayed / be gone

14 "Would you like some coffee?"
"I'd rather ... some tea."
- a/ have
- b/ to have
- c/ had
- d/ I had

15 He'd better ... in new equipment.
- a/ to invest
- b/ invest
- c/ had invested
- d/ to have invested

16 There's no answer when I call them: they ... be away.
- a/ can
- b/ must
- c/ should
- d/ are allowed to

17 Pedestrians should ... careful when crossing a street.
- a/ had been
- b/ were
- c/ be
- d/ to be

18 He ought ... from his job.
- a/ had resigned
- b/ would resign
- c/ resign
- d/ to resign

19 They ... downtown, so they stayed at home.
- a/ wouldn't need go
- b/ needn't have gone
- c/ didn't need to go
- d/ didn't need go

20 We ... at home to wait for them for they didn't come.
- a/ wouldn't have stayed
- b/ needn't have stayed
- c/ didn't need to stay
- d/ didn't need stay

1 Education

The American educational system is based on the belief that a child is naturally good. Hence the stress laid on self-discipline in American schools.
But the Americans also believe that the child may be improved by the use of appropriate teaching methods.

1 The goals of education
In order to give all children, in theory at least, equal opportunities, education is free and compulsory.
To prepare them for adult life, the emphasis is laid on practical knowledge, observation, experiments and a permanent dialogue between teacher and pupils.
Education is also supposed to turn the children into good American citizens.
Finally, the Americans insist on the fact that a child should feel happy at school.

2 The educational system
An American child is required to attend school up to the age of 17 or 18, depending on where he lives. Though there are private schools, most children attend a comprehensive coeducational public school.
Small children usually go to nursery-school or kindergarten; then, at the age of 6, they enter elementary school.
At the age of 11, they go to junior high school, then to senior high school.
When they have obtained their High School Diploma (at 17), they may follow classes as Undergraduates in a College of Liberal Arts, for four years.
After graduating, i.e. obtaining their Bachelor's Degree, the students may go to university as graduates. There, they will take their Master's Degree, and, later, their Ph. D.

3 The Federal Office and local control
Though the Federal Office of Education gives general directions as well as financial help, local control is very important and gives rise to major differences. For instance, the educational level is lower in poor districts where the Boards of Education have limited financial means at their disposal.
Moreover, many parents cannot afford to send their children to university where education is not free.
Thus full equality remains a myth, not a reality.

MODERN AMERICA

hence	d'où
the **stress** (= **em**phasis) laid on	l'accent mis sur

1

a **goal**	un but
equal **op**por**tu**nities	des chances égales
free and com**pul**sory	gratuite et obligatoire

2

is re**qui**red to	doit
a **public school** (1)	US : une école publique
coedu**ca**tional	mixte
compre**hen**sive **school**	école où se retrouvent tous les types d'enseignement secondaire
kinder**gar**ten	jardin d'enfants, école maternelle
an **Un**der**gra**duate	un étudiant qui n'a pas encore de diplôme universitaire
College	université (US)
i.e. = **id est** = **that** is	c'est-à-dire

3

to **give rise** to	faire naître
a **Board** of Edu**ca**tion	une commission locale élue chargée du recrutement des professeurs, du budget, etc...
cannot af**ford** to	ne peuvent se permettre de
thus	ainsi

OTHER WORDS AND PHRASES

a **board**ing-school	un pensionnat
a **teach**ers' **train**ing **coll**ege	une école normale
a **lec**ture	une conférence, un cours magistral
the three R's = **Read**ing, **Writ**ing, **A**rithmetic	la lecture, l'écriture, le calcul (2)
a re**qui**red **sub**ject	une matière obligatoire
an e**lect**ive or **op**tional **sub**ject	une matière facultative
the curriculum	le programme (des études)
a **schol**arship	une bourse
a **Fresh**man	un étudiant de 1re année
a **So**phomore	un étudiant de 2e année
a **Jun**ior	un étudiant de 3e année
a **Sen**ior	un étudiant de 4e année
an **alum**nus (masc.) an **alum**na (fém.)	ancien(ne) élève
alma **ma**ter	l'université à laquelle on a appartenu
a **school drop**-out	quelqu'un qui a abandonné ses études

---

1. G.B. : école privée.
2. On désigne ainsi l'enseignement de base de l'école élémentaire.

2   The American family

The basic cell of social life in the United States is "the nuclear family." It is a two-generation family, including parents and children, separated from a larger kingroup (grandparents, in-laws, uncles, and aunts).

1   The mother
Most American women give up their jobs when they become mothers. They devote themselves to the upbringing of their children and therefore play a prominent part in the life of the family.

In the morning, after preparing breakfast for the whole family, the mother drives the children to school in her own car. Then she is free to organize her day.

With the help of innumerable domestic appliances, she goes through the household tasks in no time at all. Shopping is done in the weekly visits to the supermarket.

The American woman therefore enjoys much free time and is expected to be active in the community: she has her clubs, her parent-teacher associations, her kaffee-klatsches.

2   The father
Contrary to his wife, the American man spends most of his time out of home. He is the "breadwinner" and his job takes quite a lot of his day.

However, in the evening, he is expected and willing to share his wife's activities. Many an American father changes the baby's diapers, helps to prepare the dinner or washes up the dishes.

He too has out-of-home activities in addition to his job: sports, clubs, or politics.

3   The children
The children's way of life is not unlike that of their parents. The latter do not try to keep the children within the family circle. On the contrary, they encourage them to have an independent life.

When school is over, children and teenagers spend much of their free time at their clubs or on athletic contests.

If they fail to mix with other young people, they will be regarded as ill-adapted to social life. It is so important to be popular!

MODERN AMERICA

a **cell**	une cellule
kingroup	membres de la famille
the **in**-laws	les beaux-parents

1

to **give up**	abandonner
to de**vote** one**self** to	se consacrer à
upbringing (1)	éducation
therefore	par conséquent
a **prominent part**	un rôle très important
in**num**erable	innombrable(s)
do**mes**tic ap**plia**nces	appareils ménagers
household tasks	travaux domestiques
in **no** time at **all**	en très peu de temps
weekly	hebdomadaire(s)
a **kaf**fee-**klatsch**	une réunion autour d'une tasse de café (2)

2

contrary to (3)	au contraire de
the "**bread**winner" (4)	celui qui gagne le pain de la famille
willing to share	disposé à partager
a **di**aper	une couche

3

is **not** un**like**	ressemble à
the **lat**ter	ces derniers
with**in**	à l'intérieur de
to **fail** to do sth.	ne pas faire qch.

re**gard**ed as	considéré comme
popular	1/ populaire 2/ apprécié, en vogue

OTHER WORDS AND PHRASES

a ma**ter**nity-hospital	une maternité
motherhood	la maternité (le fait d'être mère)
to **lie in**, to give **birth** to a **child**	accoucher
I was **born** on ...	je suis né (e) le ...
to **rear**, to **bring** up **child**ren	élever des enfants
well-**bred**	bien élevé
ill-**bred**	mal élevé
naughty	méchant (enfant)
to **spoil** a **child**	gâter un enfant
to **scold**	gronder
to for**give**	pardonner
daily **life**	la vie quotidienne
to **get up**	se lever
to **wash**	se laver
to **dress**	s'habiller
to **shave**	se raser
to **make up** one's **face**	se maquiller
a **meal**	un repas

---

1. Formé sur **to bring up** : élever (des enfants).
2. Réunion pendant laquelle les femmes discutent de leurs enfants, de la communauté, etc...
3. Attention ! **On the contrary** : au contraire.
4. Attention ! Ne pas traduire : gagne-pain !

3 American women

1 Marriage
By her education, by tradition, and also by women's magazines, an American girl is encouraged to consider marriage and motherhood as the sole purpose of her life.
She therefore devotes much of her time, as a teenager, to the search for a suitable husband. She may have several dates, or boyfriends, without incurring reproaches. The more dates she has, the more popular she is considered to be.
Eventually, she may go steady with a boy, get engaged and finally marry him.

2 The traditional image
After her marriage, the life of the average American woman will be centered on the home and the community.
To her children she will simply be "Mom". But, in fact, she will be the true mistress of the household, running the home and the family and holding the purse-strings. To her husband will fall the part of "breadwinner".
When her children have reached school-age, she will take a very active part in the life of the community by joining clubs and participating in welfare activities.

3 The Women's Liberation Movement (Women's Lib)
This traditional image has been denounced by the leaders of the feminist movement (Betty Friedan, Gloria Steiner, etc...). According to the women's libbers, women should no longer be subservient to their husbands. They should be offered the same opportunities as men.
The movement struggles against sexual discrimination at work. It demands the possibility for women to accede to key posts as well as to the blue-collar jobs hitherto reserved for men. Among its main preoccupations are issues of paramount interest for working women: equal pay, day-care centres, maternity benefits, contraception and abortion.
Thus, by fighting steadily for the eradication of sex discrimination, the movement has been playing an extremely positive part. Its main achievement is probably to have led women to reconsider their own role in society.

MODERN AMERICA

1

motherhood	la maternité (le fait d'être mère)
the sole purpose	le seul but
a teenager	un(e) adolescent(e) (âgé de 13 à 19 ans)
the search for	la recherche de
suitable	convenable
a date	1 / un rendez-vous 2 / personne avec qui on a rendez-vous
to incur	encourir
eventually (1)	en fin de compte
to go steady with	sortir régulièrement avec
to get engaged	se fiancer
to marry somebody (2)	épouser quelqu'un

2

to hold the purse-strings	tenir les cordons de la bourse
will fall the part of	incombera le rôle de
welfare activities	activités bénévoles dans le domaine social

3

denounced	dénoncé
according to	selon
subservient t	subordonné(es) à
to struggle	lutter
to accede to	accéder à
a key post	un poste important
as well as	ainsi que
a blue-collar job (3)	un travail manuel dans l'industrie
hitherto	jusqu'ici
main	principal(e)
an issue	une question, un problème
of paramount interest	du plus grand intérêt
a day-care centre	une crèche ou une garderie
maternity benefits	allocations de grossesse et de maternité
abortion	avortement
steadily	fermement et sans relâche
eradication	la suppression radicale
an achievement	une réussite

OTHER WORDS AND PHRASES

a domestic appliance	un appareil ménager
wash-and-wear clothes	vêtements qui ne se repassent pas
canned food (US) = tinned food (GB)	conserves
processed food	plats cuisinés
a male chauvinist	un sexiste, un phallocrate
a temporary job	un travail temporaire
a part-time job	un travail à mi-temps
a career woman	femme qui préfère son métier au mariage

---

1. Faux-ami ! « Éventuellement » : **possibly, on occasion, should the occasion arise.**
2. Se marier : **to get married.**
3. **A white-collar job** : un travail de bureau.

4 Leisure

1 The leisure society
In the past, leisure used to be the privilege of the upper classes. But, with the rising standard of living, it has become available to the masses.

The five-day week has replaced the six-day week, and the four-day week may not be very far away.

Though many American workers do not yet enjoy four-week holidays, a leisure ethic has gradually replaced the old Protestant Work Ethic.

With the expansion of leisure, new industries have developed. Their purpose is to produce goods that people use in their free time. This means automobiles, of course, but also sports equipment, camping equipment, etc...

Many services cater for the demand for organized leisure (travel agents, for instance).

2 Spare-time activities
Going for a walk is rather unusual owing to the size of the cities and sprawling suburbs. America has become "a civilization on wheels" (Max Lerner) and the automobile is therefore the key to many entertainments. This is often rendered necessary by the lay-out of the cities, towns and suburbs. Thus drive-in movies, drive-in shopping centres have developed.

Yet many leisure-time occupations do not require considerable expenditure. Many Americans enjoy pottering about the house, doing odd jobs, in order to improve their home.

American people also entertain a great deal. They do not give formal dinners but casual parties at which the guests eat sandwiches or dishes that are easy to prepare.

Outdoor games are very popular in the States, in particular baseball, the American adaptation of the English cricket. As to the bicycle, it has recently experienced renewed popularity.

The sales figures of "paperbacks" in the U.S. suggest that some people devote part of their free time to reading. However, it is worth pointing out that, here again, advertising plays an enormous role: many Americans buy and read the books advertised as "best-sellers", thus conforming to the tastes of the majority.

MODERN AMERICA

leisure	les loisirs

1

the **ri**sing **stand**ard of **liv**ing	la montée du niveau de vie
a**vail**able to	accessible à
a **lei**sure **e**thic	une éthique des loisirs (1)
to **cat**er for	pourvoir à

2

spare-time	loisirs (temps libre)
owing to	à cause de
sprawling	très étendu
en**ter**tainments	distractions
the **lay**-out	le plan, le tracé
a **drive**-in **mov**ie	un cinéma en plein air (2)
ex**pen**diture	dépenses
to **pot**ter about the **house** = to do **odd jobs**	bricoler
to enter**tain**	recevoir
formal	cérémonieux
casual	sans cérémonies, simple
outdoor **games**	les jeux de plein air, les activités sportives
the **sales** figures	les chiffres de vente
a **pa**perback	un livre broché (3)
it is **worth** pointing out	il est à remarquer
a **best**-seller	un livre qui se vend bien (4)
to con**form** to	se conformer à

OTHER WORDS AND PHRASES
---

a **pas**time	un passe-temps
a **hob**by	un violon d'Ingres
an **e**vent	une rencontre sportive
a **team**	une équipe
the **um**pire	l'arbitre
winter **sports**	les sports d'hiver
swimming	la natation
a **swim**ming-pool	une piscine
indoor **games**	les jeux d'intérieur
reading	la lecture
a **thrill**er	un roman à sensation
a de**tec**tive novel	un roman policier
amateur dra**ma**tics	le théâtre d'amateurs
a **ci**ne camera	une caméra
a **cam**era	un appareil photographique
the **screen**	l'écran
the **au**dience	le public
the di**rec**tor	le metteur en scène
a car**toon**	1 / un dessin humoristique 2 / un dessin animé
a **mov**ie-goer	un amateur de cinéma
to en**joy** oneself	s'amuser
to en**joy** sth.	profiter, jouir de qch.
to be **bored**	s'ennuyer

1. Par opposition à l'éthique protestante du travail (**Protestant Work Ethic**).
2. On regarde le film sans sortir de voiture.
3. Livre du type de nos livres de poche.
4. Des listes de best-sellers sont publiées toutes les semaines dans les hebdomadaires américains.

5 The mass media

The <u>mass media</u>: the press, the radio and television, have a <u>widespread</u> influence in the United States. They <u>mould</u> the opinions of a large section of the population and are, <u>to some extent,</u> responsible for the standardization of American life and of mass culture.

1 The press
Though the <u>advent</u> of television <u>brought about</u> the disappearance of many newspapers, the press still plays a major role. In addition to reporting political events, it is expected <u>to disclose</u> facts unknown to <u>the public at large.</u> The Watergate affair, which <u>eventually</u> led to President Nixon's <u>resignation</u>, <u>testified to</u> the importance of the press.
It is <u>significant</u> that the freedom of the press should have been attacked by some presidential administrations.

2 Television
Television, which is <u>ubiquitous</u> in America, has <u>driven</u> all the other media <u>into the background</u>. By keeping people at home <u>it has been prejudicial to</u> almost all other forms of entertainment, some of which have been adapted to the TV <u>screen</u> (thus the drama, and the movie).
Its potential is enormous and it could certainly be a superb means of education. Marshall McLuhan called it "the classroom without walls".

3 Television under attack
To understand the attacks against this medium, it is necessary <u>to bear in mind</u> the use that is or can be made of it. Television is often <u>charged with</u> <u>indoctrinating</u> the masses or at least <u>lowering</u> intellectual standards.
Besides, the programmes are, <u>more often than not,</u> very <u>poor.</u> American television <u>belongs to</u> private owners and its profits depend on advertising. "<u>Commercials</u>" constantly interrupt the programmes.
As a matter of fact, very few people watch television <u>discriminatingly</u> or demand better quality programmes. Most <u>viewers</u> are <u>content with</u> <u>quizz shows,</u> westerns, and <u>thrillers</u>; they do not care if television is used as a means <u>to bias people's opinions.</u>

MODERN AMERICA

the **mass me**dia (1)	les moyens de communication de masse
widespread	étendu(e)
to **mould**	façonner
to some ex**tent**	dans une certaine mesure

1

ad**vent**	apparition
to **bring about**	entraîner, causer
to dis**close**	révéler
the **pub**lic at **large**	le public dans son ensemble
resig**na**tion	démission
to **tes**tify to	témoigner de
sig**ni**ficant	significatif

2

u**bi**quitous	omniprésent(e)
to **drive into** the **back**ground	prendre le pas sur
to be **pre**judicial to	nuire à
screen	écran

3

to **bear** in **mind**	ne pas oublier
to be **charged** with	être accusé(e) de
to in**doc**trinate	endoctriner
to **low**er	abaisser
more **of**ten than **not**	le plus souvent
poor	médiocre
to be**long** to	appartenir à
a com**mer**cial	une annonce publicitaire
dis**cri**minatingly	avec discernement
a **view**er	un téléspectateur
to be con**tent** with	se contenter de
a **quizz** show	un jeu radiophonique ou télévisé
a **thrill**er	un livre ou film à sensation
to **bi**as **peo**ple's o**pi**nions	fausser les opinions des gens

---

OTHER WORDS AND PHRASES

the **ads**	les petites annonces
a **co**mic strip	une bande dessinée
a **dai**ly	un quotidien
a **week**ly	un hebdomadaire
a **se**rial	un feuilleton
the **news**	les actualités
a **news**-boy	un vendeur de journaux
a **news**-stand	un kiosque à journaux
a **te**levision **set**	un poste de télévision
broadcasting	radio- ou télé-diffusion
to **broad**cast a **sport**ing e**vent**	retransmettre une rencontre sportive

---

1. Singulier : **a medium.**

6 Music

American people are very fond of music. Most American households own at least one record-player and a tape-recorder.

1 Classical music

About fifty per cent of the records sold in the U.S. are classical music.

Many cities have first-rate orchestras and foreign conductors often come to America to make a career. Many great musicians of our time have lived or are living in the U.S. though the country cannot pride itself on a high number of national composers with world-wide fame.

2 Jazz

Jazz, which is characterized by improvisation and strong rhythms, is the pre-eminently American variety of music. It is in fact the Americanized interpretation of African music.

The slaves used to sing *blues* expressing their revolt or their melancholy. The Negro *spirituals* were Protestant religious songs influenced by African musical traditions. The *work songs,* sung by Negro labourers and by convicts, had strong rhythms inspired by working gestures. And it was *dance music* which was first called jazz.

Jazz was born in Louisiana, particularly in New Orleans, in the latter half of the 19th century.

Until 1920 it remained exclusively in the Negro night-clubs. After this date, during the "jazz age", it came to Saint Louis, Harlem, and Chicago.

Thanks to talented musicians, it asserted itself as the national music of the U.S. and one of the basic forms of contemporary art.

3 Songs

American songs have become a consumer item whose evolution has been similar to that of European songs. But they are more rhythmical and more violent in their words and tunes.

The appearance of committed singers, together with a revived interest in folk songs, has renewed the American song over the past few years.

But even these new trends cannot remain free from the tentacular influence of show business.

a **house**hold	un foyer
to **own**	posséder
a **re**cord-player	un électrophone
a **ta**pe-recorder	un magnétophone

1

first-**rate**	de premier ordre
a con**duc**tor	un chef d'orchestre
to **pride** oneself on	s'enorgueillir de
world-wide **fame**	renommée mondiale

2

pre-**e**minently	par excellence
a **con**vict	un forçat
a **ges**ture	un geste
the **latter half**	la seconde moitié
thanks to	grâce à
to as**sert** one**self**	s'affirmer, s'imposer

3

a con**su**mer **i**tem	un produit de consommation
the **tune**	l'air (la mélodie)
com**mit**ted	engagé
to**ge**ther with	en même temps que
a **trend**	une tendance
show business = **show biz**	l'industrie du spectacle

OTHER WORDS AND EXPRESSIONS
---

to **have** the **blues**	avoir le cafard
to **play** the **pia**no, the **vi**olin, the gui**tar**	jouer du piano, du violon, de la guitare
the **strings**	les instruments à cordes
the **brass**	les cuivres
the **wind**	les instruments à vent
the **big drum** = the **bass drum**	la grosse caisse
the **ket**tle-drum	la timbale
a **band** (1)	un orchestre
a **trap**	un groupe d'instruments à percussion
the **drum**mer	le batteur
the **key**board (of a piano)	le clavier
a **key**	une touche
to **key** up the **strings** of an **ins**trument	accorder un instrument à cordes
to **tune** a **pia**no	accorder un piano
a **croon**er (2)	un chanteur de charme
a **mike** = a **mic**rophone	un micro(phone)
A, B, C, D, E, F, G	la, si, do, ré, mi, fa, sol

---

1. Noter que l'on dit **jazz band** mais **philharmonic orchestra**.
2. Vient de **to croon** : fredonner, chanter à mi-voix. Frank Sinatra est le type même du **crooner**.

Grammar and exercises

"Tags"
(Phrases elliptiques)

"Tags" correspondant au français **MOI AUSSI** (toi, lui... aussi).

— *Il est en retard.* — *Moi aussi.*

"He is late." **"So am I."**

— *Les Smith sont allés à Paris.* — *Les Jones aussi.*

"The Smiths went to Paris." **"So did the Joneses."**

— *Je jouerai au tennis demain.* — *John aussi.*

"I'll play tennis tomorrow." **"So will John."**

Noter qu'un verbe ordinaire au présent ou au prétérit est rappelé par l'auxiliaire DO conjugué, un verbe conjugué avec un auxiliaire par cet auxiliaire.

"Tags" correspondant au français **MOI NON PLUS**

— *Je n'ai pas de voiture.* — *Moi non plus.*

"I haven't got a car." **"Neither have I."**

— *Je n'irai pas à Paris l'été prochain.* — *Peter non plus.*

"I won't go to Paris next summer." **"Neither will Peter."**

— *Nous n'aimons pas voyager.* — *Eux non plus.*

"We don't like travelling." **"Neither do they."**

Autre construction possible avec **either** :

— *Je n'aime pas conduire.* — *Moi non plus.*

"I don't like driving." **"I don't either."**

— *Je ne vais pas à la campagne demain.* — *Lui non plus.*

"I'm not going to the country tomorrow." **"He isn't either."**

MODERN AMERICA 71

A *React to the first sentence, using the pronoun or noun in brackets, as in the following example:*

Ex.: a/ "My children are back from school." (mine)
→ b/ "So are mine."

1 a/ "Our son will go to College next year." (ours)
2 a/ "We might go to the country if it does not rain." (we)
3 a/ "He passed his Master's Degree a year ago." (John)
4 a/ "Fortunately we can afford to send our daughter to university." (the Wilsons)
5 a/ "Next year, Mary will be a Sophomore." (Joan)
6 a/ "I would give up my job if I had a child." (I)
7 a/ "He has been working all day." (Mr Jones)
8 a/ "I wish I had more free time." (all working women)
9 a/ "Obviously she had considered marriage as the sole purpose of her life." (all the women of her generation)
10 a/ "You should be less subservient to your husband." (most women)

B *React to the first sentence, using the pronoun or noun in brackets, as in the following example:*

Ex.: a/ "My children are not back from school." (mine)
→ b/ "Neither are mine."
  c/ "Mine aren't either."

1 a/ "Mary has not found a suitable husband after all." (Joan)
2 a/ "Mrs Smith didn't give up her job when she had a baby." (Mrs Wilson)
3 a/ "Jane shouldn't be subservient to her husband." (you)
4 a/ "I wouldn't like to live in the country." (I)
5 a/ "If I had known better, I wouldn't have married a male chauvinist."(I)
6 a/ "Because I'm a woman I couldn't obtain a key post." (I)
7 a/ "Though she is a feminist, she doesn't want to be given a blue-collar job." (most women)
8 a/ "We hadn't expected the President to resign." (most Americans)
9 a/ "He didn't speak the truth." (you)
10 a/ "She won't be here early." (my wife)

Question tag (= français N'EST-CE PAS?)

Phrase affirmative → **Question tag négatif**
— *Il est très vieux, n'est-ce pas?*
   He is very old, isn't he?

— *Vous viendrez, n'est-ce pas?*
   You'll come, won't you?

— *Ils sont allés à Manchester, n'est-ce pas?*
   They went to Manchester, didn't they?

Phrase négative → **Question tag affirmatif**
— *Vous ne partez pas, n'est-ce pas?*
   You are not leaving, are you?

— *Ils ne viendront pas, n'est-ce pas?*
   They won't come, will they?

— *Elle n'est pas fâchée, n'est-ce pas?*
   She is not cross, is she?

Inversion sujet-verbe

Pour insister sur un terme négatif, restrictif ou intensif, on peut le placer au début de la phrase. Cette tournure entraîne l'inversion de la construction sujet-verbe :

— **Never shall we forget** what you did for us.
   (Jamais nous n'oublierons ce que vous avez fait pour nous.)

— **Not once did he say** that he would help us.
   (Pas une seule fois il n'a dit qu'il nous aiderait.)

— **Seldom have I seen** such a brute.
   (C'est bien rarement que j'ai vu une telle brute.)

MODERN AMERICA

A *Complete the following sentences with the appropriate question tag as in the two following examples:*

Ex.: a/ I told you the whole story, ...
→ b/ I told you the whole story, didn't I?
or: a/ They haven't called, ...
→ b/ They haven't called, have they?

1 American children attend school up to the age of 17 or 18, ...?
2 In the States, education is free, ...?
3 You bought a new vacuum-cleaner yesterday, ...?
4 They have encouraged their children to be independent, ...?
5 This child could join our club, ...?
6 She hadn't had her baby yet when she gave up her job, ...?
7 If they don't mix with other people, they won't be regarded as well-adapted to social life, ...?
8 She couldn't have worked harder than she did, ...?
9 You have never been very fond of winter sports, ...?
10 It won't be a very formal dinner, ...?

B *Reword the following sentences, putting the underlined word or phrase at the beginning of the sentence or clause:*

1 Leisure activities will <u>never</u> be accessible to the underprivileged.
2 You did <u>not</u> go <u>once</u> to a drive-in movie when you were in the States.
3 She can <u>not only</u> look after five children but she also has a key post in a big company.
4 She knew <u>little</u> how happy she was then.
5 She had <u>no sooner</u> spoken than he came in.
6 I have <u>vainly</u> tried to improve my position at the office.
7 The children are <u>nowhere</u> to be found.
8 We'll be able to leave <u>only when she is ready</u>.
9 The party gave them <u>so little pleasure</u> that they were sorry they had gone.
10 I <u>never</u> said such a thing.

Exclamations

ADJECTIFS ET ADVERBES
3 possibilités :
— She is so beautiful!
— How beautiful she is!
— Isn't she beautiful! (ton plus familier)

NOMS
1°/ Dénombrable au singulier :
— **What a** lovely house!
— It is **such a** lovely house!

2°/ Dénombrable au pluriel :
— **What** lovely houses there are in this village!
— There are **such** lovely houses in this village!

3°/ Indénombrable au singulier :
— **What** pride he showed!
— He showed **such** pride!

Noter qu'il n'y a pas d'inversion sujet-verbe.

Constructions particulières : dans les tournures exclamatives, on emploie l'article indéfini entre **what** ou **such** et les indénombrables suivants : **hurry, fuss, relief, pity** (signifiant « dommage »), **shame, disgrace,** et **mess.**
— What a hurry you are in! *(Que vous êtes pressé!)*
— She made such a fuss about it! *(Que d'embarras...)*
— What a relief to find out that you are well *(Quel soulagement...)*
— What a pity you can't come! *(Quel dommage...)*
— What a shame! *(Quelle honte! ou : Quel dommage!)*
— What a disgrace for the family! *(Quelle honte...)*
— She's made such a mess of the whole thing! *(Quel gâchis...)*

Exclamations portant sur la quantité :
— What a lot of money you have!
— What a lot of flowers there are in the garden!

MODERN AMERICA

A *Turn the following sentences into exclamatory sentences as in the examples:*

Ex.: a / Peter is a <u>bright</u> undergraduate.
→ b / Peter is so bright.
c / How bright Peter is!
d / Isn't Peter bright!

or: a / Peter is a bright <u>undergraduate</u>.
b / What a bright undergraduate Peter is!
c / Peter is such a bright undergraduate!

1 a / This detective novel is really <u>interesting</u>.
2 a / Mary is a devoted <u>movie-goer</u>.
3 a / Their parties are always very <u>formal</u>.
4 a / He is an excellent <u>actor</u>.
5 a / The mass media have a widespread <u>influence</u>.
6 a / The freedom of the press is very <u>important</u>.
7 a / TV commercials really are <u>a nuisance</u>.
8 a / He showed great <u>courage</u> in that ordeal.

B *Use the indefinite article when necessary:*

1 What ... event the advent of television was!
2 What ... pity so many people should be besotted by TV!
3 He showed such ... pity for the children of developing nations!
4 What ... stupid show that was!
5 What ... disgrace to the country the TV programmes are!
6 What ... lot of records are sold in the U.S. every year!
7 He is such ... great musician! He has such ... talent!
8 This is such ... beautiful negro spiritual!

Test

1 "John is going to London tomorrow."   "..."
  ☐ a/ So am I.
  ☐ b/ So do I.
  ☐ c/ So will I.
  ☐ d/ So shall I.

2 "We had saved a lot of money to buy our house."   "..."
  ☐ a/ So are we.
  ☐ b/ So did we.
  ☐ c/ So have we.
  ☐ d/ So had we.

3 "She took a part-time job two years ago."   "..."
  ☐ a/ So are you.
  ☐ b/ So did you.
  ☐ c/ So have you.
  ☐ d/ So had you.

4 "They would like their children to get the best education."   "..."
  ☐ a/ So are we.
  ☐ b/ So did we.
  ☐ c/ So we would.
  ☐ d/ So would we.

5 "You must work harder if you want to pass your exam."   "..."
  ☐ a/ So must you.
  ☐ b/ So will you
  ☐ c/ So do you
  ☐ d/ So have you.

6 We could go to the swimming-pool, and ....
  ☐ a/ so would you
  ☐ b/ so could you
  ☐ c/ so will you
  ☐ d/ so you could

7 I wouldn't like to live in the country, and ....
  ☐ a/ he wouldn't neither
  ☐ b/ neither wouldn't he
  ☐ c/ neither would he
  ☐ d/ neither he would

8 "I haven't got any hobby."   "..."
  ☐ a/ Neither have I
  ☐ b/ Neither me
  ☐ c/ Either have I.
  ☐ d/ Either I have

9 "He wouldn't do it even if he could."   "..."
  ☐ a/ Neither I would
  ☐ b/ Either would I
  ☐ c/ I wouldn't either
  ☐ d/ Neither wouldn't I

MODERN AMERICA

10 They cannot go to the seaside next summer, and ....
- a/ we can neither
- b/ we can't either
- c/ we can either
- d/ neither we can

11 She doesn't work in an office, ...?
- a/ is she
- b/ does she
- c/ doesn't she
- d/ isn't she

12 They are coming tomorrow, ...?
- a/ do they
- b/ won't they
- c/ aren't they
- d/ are they

13 They have gone to London, ...?
- a/ have they
- b/ haven't they
- c/ did they
- d/ didn't they

14 You will never forget what they did for you, ...?
- a/ will you
- b/ do you
- c/ won't you
- d/ aren't you

15 Never ... forget that day!
- a/ we'll
- b/ we shall
- c/ we will
- d/ shall we

16 Seldom ... on us over the past few months.
- a/ they called
- b/ did they call
- c/ have they called
- d/ they have called

17 Nowhere ... as many opportunities as in the States.
- a/ you find
- b/ you found
- c/ do you find
- d/ you have found

18 ... selfishness he showed!
- a/ What
- b/ What a
- c/ How
- d/ How many

19 How well-bred ...!
- a/ your children are
- b/ are your children
- c/ your children do
- d/ will your children

20 ... good schools there are in your district!
- a/ How
- b/ How much
- c/ What
- d/ What a

A *Translate into English:*

1 — Je crois que les enfants sont naturellement bons. — Moi aussi.
2 Elle est allée à l'école jusqu'à l'âge de 18 ans, et son frère aussi.
3 — Il faut que je fasse mes devoirs. — Ton frère aussi.
4 — Peter aimerait bien jouer au tennis. — Moi aussi.
5 — Nous pouvons nous permettre d'envoyer nos enfants à l'université. — Nous aussi.
6 Quand j'ai quitté l'université, j'y suivais des cours depuis 6 ans, et mon mari aussi.
7 — Que fait Mary en ce moment? — Elle travaille, et son frère en fait autant.
8 — J'assisterai à la conférence du professeur Wilson demain. — Moi aussi.
9 Mes parents n'habitent pas avec nous, et mes beaux-parents non plus.
10 — Elle n'aimerait pas abandonner son travail pour son mari. — Moi non plus.
11 — Nous n'avions pas beaucoup d'argent quand nous nous sommes mariés. — Nous non plus.
12 — Ils sont américains mais ils ne sont pas nés aux États-Unis. — Nous non plus.

B *Translate into English:*

1 Leurs enfants sont bien élevés, n'est-ce pas?
2 Elle n'a jamais envisagé de travailler, n'est-ce pas?
3 Quand elle s'est mariée, elle n'avait jamais eu de situation, n'est-ce pas?
4 Vous prendrez la voiture pour aller faire vos courses, n'est-ce pas?
5 Votre mari a toujours aimé bricoler dans la maison, n'est-ce pas?
6 Il n'y a pas beaucoup de gens qui occupent leurs loisirs à lire, n'est-ce pas?
7 Si vous en aviez le temps, vous liriez plus, n'est-ce pas?
8 Votre petit garçon ne s'ennuie jamais, n'est-ce pas?

C *Translate into English:*

1 Jamais je n'achèterai un poste de télévision!
2 Non seulement ils n'ont pas de livres chez eux, mais ils en sont fiers!
3 C'est seulement en 1920 que le jazz est venu à Chicago.
4 Pas une seule fois ce chanteur n'a chanté sans micro.
5 C'est bien rarement qu'un enfant des classes défavorisées fait des études brillantes.
6 Il ne travaille pas bien à l'école, et il n'est pas très agréable à la maison.
7 « A aucun prix je n'enverrais ma fille dans une école mixte », a dit la vieille dame.
8 Plus jamais les femmes n'accepteront d'être les domestiques de leur mari.
9 Ils n'étaient pas plus tôt sortis se promener qu'il commença à pleuvoir.
10 Nulle part les soirées ne sont aussi agréables que chez les Martin.
11 Jamais plus je ne lui parlerai!
12 Non seulement il est en retard, mais il ne s'excuse même pas!

D *Translate into English:*

1 Quel talent a ce chef d'orchestre!
2 Comme vous êtes pressé!
3 Que cette chanson est jolie!
4 Que de musiciens contemporains vivent aux États-Unis!
5 Quel soulagement d'apprendre que l'accident n'a pas été grave!
6 Quel dommage que nous ne puissions aller à ce concert!
7 Quelle belle chose que l'instruction!
8 Que ces enfants sont mignons!
9 Quelle honte pour la famille!
10 Que le niveau des études est bas dans cette école!

1 Protestantism and the Work Ethic

1 Protestantism and Capitalism

Some sociologists believe that certain trends of Protestantism, especially Calvinism, have facilitated the development of capitalism in the northwest of Europe. From there, it went to the U.S. with the immigrants.

Indeed, for Calvin, faith and daily life are closely linked: doing one's best in one's work is a way to serve God.

As a consequence, success in one's work may be considered as the sign of God's approval.

The Americans have inherited from the Puritans the belief in the truth of such notions.

2 The Work Ethic

Hence the American belief that work is a kind of religious duty and that efficiency carries its own moral justification. Moreover, the Americans cherish the idea that every man can rise in society by dint of hard work. To prove this assertion, they willingly cite the example of the great barons of industry who were self-made men.

Such beliefs undoubtedly give American society its remarkable vitality, since many people act to the best of their abilities. To the Work Ethic the U.S. owes the fact that it is a nation of inventors and entrepreneurs.

In this approach to life, work deserves a fair reward: this reward is money. Therefore, earning money is morally valuable, it is even a token of morality.

3 The distortions of the Work Ethic

As a consequence of this attitude, many Americans, and the U.S. itself, have been led to consider actions as moral if they are useful to them.

Besides, Americans tend to consider that the man who does not work is guilty, whatever the national economic situation may be. Thus the unemployed are regarded by many as lazy and even immoral people. Many Americans consider that the dole (the unemployment benefit) is an inducement to laziness. They even question the necessity of a Welfare State. Ex-President Nixon said very plainly that he believed in the Work Ethic, not in the Welfare Ethic.

the Work Ethic — l'éthique du travail

1

a trend	une tendance
faith	la foi
daily life	la vie quotidienne
approval	approbation
to inherit sth. from someone	hériter qch. de qqn.

2

hence	d'où
a duty	un devoir
efficiency	l'efficacité
to carry	porter
moreover	de plus
to cherish an idea	être très attaché à une idée
by dint of	à force de
an assertion	une affirmation
willingly	volontiers
a baron (of industry)	un capitaine d'industrie
undoubtedly	sans aucun doute
to owe	devoir
in this approach to life	selon cette conception de la vie
to deserve	mériter
fair	juste
reward	récompense
therefore	donc
even	même
a token	un signe

3

a distortion	une déformation
have been led to	ont été conduits à
besides	d'autre part, de plus
to tend to	avoir tendance à
guilty	coupable
thus	ainsi
to regard	considérer
the dole = the unemployment benefit	l'allocation chômage
an inducement	un encouragement
to question	contester, mettre en doute
the Welfare State	l'État Providence (1)
plainly	simplement

---

1. L'État Providence est celui qui prend en charge le bien-être des citoyens.

2 Business

The business organization is a basic structure in America, and its influence continues to spread throughout the country.
The big corporations have given the U.S. its specificity and made it the model which all capitalist industrialized countries look up to.

1 The business organization
A corporation does not belong to an individual; it belongs to the shareholders; every share represents a portion of the capital of the firm.
The activities of the company are supervised by the Board of Directors. The chairman is the head of the company.
The various executives see to the smooth working of their departments and are in direct contact with the personnel.
When a company expands, branches are opened up in other cities.
A company with branches all over the world is a multinational.

2 Big Business
The Standard Oil Company was the first business combination: it is called the "mother" of trusts.
A merger results from the desire either to control firms carrying on the same type of business (horizontal combination), or to control all the processes of production and marketing of a product (vertical combination).
Trusts and cartels are the results of business combinations. Holdings and pools are organizations for the financial control of various companies.

3 The seamy side of Big Business
Though big corporations are said to have brought affluence to the country, many people are now aware of the dangers inherent in their very existence.
Their power enables them to crush smaller companies. Afterwards, when they have achieved monopoly (i.e. complete control of one type of production by one firm) or oligopoly (i.e. complete control of one type of production by a small number of firms), they can fix the prices with no fear of being challenged. The consumers have to foot the bill, and the anti-trust laws are of no avail.

THE AFFLUENT SOCIETY

to **spread**	s'étendre
a corpo**ra**tion	une grosse société
speci**fi**city	originalité
to **look** up to	respecter, admirer

1

a **share**holder	un actionnaire
a **share**	1/ une part 2/ une action
the **Board** of Di**rec**tors	le Conseil d'Administration
a di**rec**tor	un administrateur
the **chair**man	le président
an e**xe**cutive	un cadre supérieur
to **see** to	veiller à, s'occuper de
the **smooth work**ing	le bon fonctionnement
a de**part**ment	un service
to ex**pand**	prendre de l'expansion
a **branch**	une filiale

2

a combi**na**tion	une concentration d'affaires
a **mer**ger	une fusion
to re**sult** from	provenir de
a **pro**cess	un processus

3

the **seamy side**	le revers de la médaille, le mauvais côté
affluence	l'abondance
to be a**ware** of	être conscient de
in**he**rent in	lié à, inhérent à
to en**a**ble	permettre
to **crush**	écraser
to a**chieve**	réussir, atteindre
mo**no**poly	le monopole
oli**go**poly	l'oligopole
a con**su**mer	un consommateur
to **foot** the **bill**	payer l'addition
to be of no a**vail**	ne servir à rien

OTHER WORDS AND PHRASES

the **head-of**fice	le siège social
a **branch-of**fice	une filiale
a **ge**neral **mee**ting	une assemblée générale
cut-throat compe**ti**tion	la compétition à mort, la lutte au couteau
free **en**terprise	la libre entreprise
to **vie** with	rivaliser avec
to **cap**ture a **mar**ket	s'emparer d'un marché

3 Wall Street

The transactions concerning shares and other securities take place in the Stock Exchange. The New York Stock Exchange is located in Wall Street, in the lower part of Manhattan.
Wall Street took its name from the palisade which was built in the 17th century to protect the Dutch settlement of New Amsterdam from an invasion by the English.

1 The working of the Stock Exchange

All trading takes place on the floor of the S E and is governed by strict rules.
Each stock is traded at only one post. Members interested in this stock congregate around this post. Some bid for the stock, others offer it for sale. Transactions are carried out in this manner.
When some particular stock is in great demand, its price rises. On the contrary, when the offers for sale are very numerous, the price of the stock falls.
The administration of the S E is vested in a Board of Governors. Candidates for membership of the S E are admitted only if their financial reputation is beyond reproach.

2 Speculation

The S E offers opportunities for speculation.
A speculator deals "for the account", which means that his transactions need not be settled until the following account-day. Since stock varies in price from one minute to the next, many changes may take place before account-day.
A "bull" is a man who acts in expectation of a rise in the price of some stock. On the contrary, the dealings of a "bear" are based upon the expectation of a drop in the price of shares.

3 The financial capital of the United States

The Wall Street area is recognized as the financial capital of the United States.
Besides the S E, all the chief financial institutions of the U.S. (the major banks and corporations) have their head-offices there.
The importance of Wall Street is not limited to the U.S. It extends to the whole capitalist world where the fluctuations of the New York Stock Exchange can be felt. This was dramatically evidenced by the world crisis of the thirties.

THE AFFLUENT SOCIETY

a **share**	une action
a se**cu**rity	un titre
the **Stock** Ex**change**	la Bourse
Dutch	hollandais

1

the **work**ing	le fonctionnement
trading	négociation
the **floor**	le "parquet"
stock	actions, valeurs
to **con**gregate	s'assembler
to **bid** for	faire une offre d'achat
to **of**fer for **sale**	faire une offre de vente
to **be** in great de**mand**	être très demandé
vested in	assigné à, exercé par
the **Board** of **Gov**ernors	le Conseil des Gouverneurs
be**yond** re**proach**	au-dessus de tout soupçon

2

to **deal** for the ac**count**	négocier à terme
to **set**tle a tran**sac**tion	régler une transaction
ac**count**-day	jour de liquidation
a "**bull**"	un haussier
in expec**ta**tion of	dans l'attente de
a **rise**	une hausse
the **deal**ings	les négociations
a "**bear**"	un baissier
a **drop** in the **price**	une baisse (du prix)

3

be**sides**	en plus de
a **head**-**of**fice	un siège social
to ex**tend** to	s'étendre à
evidenced	démontré
the **thir**ties	les années 30

OTHER WORDS AND PHRASES

a **stock**holder	un porteur de titres
a **stock**-**bro**ker	un agent de change
a **clerk**	un commis
to **dab**ble on the S E	boursicoter
to **gam**ble on the S E	jouer à la bourse
the **tone** of the **mar**ket	les dispositions de la bourse
a **flur**ry on the S E	une panique à la bourse
rigging of the **mar**ket	tripotage en bourse
a **tip**	un "tuyau"

4 Industry

The Americans' innate taste for pragmatism did much to boost the development of their industrial and technological society.

1 The importance of technology

The Americans are always wary of theories and appraise the value of an idea in terms of its material applications. For them, the "know-how" is what counts. Hence the emphasis laid on applied science.

Industries often have their own laboratories and employ full-time scientists who carry on research on their behalf.

The advance of the Americans in the field of technology is such that observers speak of a technological gap between the U.S. and the rest of the world.

2 Mass production

Though work had been standardized in some factories as early as 1840, Ford is generally considered as the industrialist who first applied the principles of Taylor on a large scale. Those principles, which aim at increased productivity, are:

a/ *Standardization:* the parts of the various models are similar and can be used in any of the models built by the factory.

b/ *Specialization:* each worker, instead of building a product from A to Z, specializes in one task. He stands at a station on the assembly-line and performs the same task.

c/ *Simplification:* this task must be simplified and repetitive to keep the line moving.

3 Man vs the Machine

Working all day under the supervision of the foreman, the blue-collar worker is deprived of the possibility of taking any initiative. Neither can he derive any pleasure from the contemplation of his work. His whole working life is doomed to anonymity. All that matters is increased productivity. This dehumanization of work is under attack from many quarters. It was effectively denounced by Charlie Chaplin in *Modern Times.* Awareness of this acute problem is such that solutions are desperately sought to try and make the job of the industrial worker less dull and more rewarding.

Indeed, when workers air their grievances or call strikes, their claims often relate to their working conditions, as much as to their wages.

THE AFFLUENT SOCIETY

innate	inné
to boost	faire progresser

1

to be wary of	se défier de
to appraise	évaluer, apprécier
know-how	savoir technique
applied	appliqué(e)
on their behalf	pour leur compte
in the field of	dans le domaine
is such that	est telle que
gap	fossé

2

industrialist	industriel
on a large scale	sur une grande échelle
to aim at	avoir pour but
a part	une pièce
a task	une tâche
a station	un poste
the assembly-line	la chaîne
to perform	accomplir
repetitive	répété(e) en série

3

vs = versus	contre
the foreman	le contremaître
the blue-collar worker	le col bleu
deprived of	privé de
neither can he derive any pleasure	et il ne peut non plus tirer aucun plaisir
doomed to	voué(e) à
anonymity	l'anonymat
all that matters	tout ce qui importe
effectively	de manière efficace
awareness	la conscience
sought ← to seek	rechercher
dull	ennuyeux
rewarding	satisfaisant
to air grievances	exprimer des doléances, des griefs
to call strikes	appeler à la grève
a claim	une revendication
to relate to	avoir trait à
wages	le(s) salaire(s)

OTHER WORDS AND PHRASES

a gang	une équipe
a shift	un changement d'équipe
a trade-union	un syndicat
dissatisfaction	insatisfaction
to work overtime	faire des heures supplémentaires
skilled workers	ouvriers qualifiés
unskilled	non qualifiés
unemployment	chômage
to be jobless	être sans travail
to be on the dole	vivre de l'indemnité chômage
to go on strike	faire grève
a picket	un piquet de grève
a blackleg	un "jaune"
a stoppage	un arrêt de travail
a demonstration	une manifestation
the working class(es)	la classe ouvrière

Grammar and exercises

Traductions de « ce que », « ce qui », « ce dont » :

1/ **what** = that which → comprend son propre antécédent et n'en a pas :
 — **what** sujet : **What** he said was most interesting.

 Ce qu'il a dit était très intéressant.

 — **what** complément : I found **what** he said most interesting.

 J'ai trouvé ce qu'il a dit très intéressant.

2/ **which**, au contraire, a pour antécédent une ou plusieurs propositions ; **which** reprend ce qui précède :
 — **which** sujet : He said he couldn't come, **which** disappointed us very much.

 Il a dit qu'il ne pourrait venir, ce qui nous a beaucoup déçus.

 — **which** complément : He said he would come another time, **which** we were all glad to hear.

 Il a dit qu'il viendrait une autre fois, ce que nous étions tous heureux d'apprendre.

Cas possessif

1/ Possesseur singulier ou pluriel irrégulier → **'s** :
 — Peter's book : *le livre de Peter.*

 — the children's books : *les livres des enfants.*

2/ Possesseur pluriel → **apostrophe seulement** :
 — the workers' difficulties : *les difficultés des travailleurs.*

3/ Cas possessif incomplet :
 — I'm going to the grocer's : *Je vais chez l'épicier.*

4/ Emploi idiomatique pour la durée et la distance :
 — a ten minutes' walk : *une promenade de dix minutes.*

 — a two miles' walk : *une promenade de deux miles.*

THE AFFLUENT SOCIETY

A *Use WHAT or WHICH in the following sentences:*

1 ... we visited during the Summer was very beautiful.
2 I don't know ... they did during the Summer.
3 Peter said his parents had gone to Spain, ... didn't surprise us.
4 I'm sure this is ... they are going to do.
5 She'll talk to her boss, ... is certainly the best thing to do.
6 The Protestant Ethic still has widespread influence in the U.S., ... accounts for some American reactions.
7 ... some sociologists say is that Protestantism has facilitated the development of capitalism.
8 He said that his wealth was the sign of God's approval of ... he does.
9 He says that wealth is the fair reward of work, ... does not always convince me.
10 ... he usually adds is that the dole is an inducement to laziness, ... convinces me even less.
11 Somebody contradicted him, ... everybody approved of.
12 This is ... we must do: open up new branches in several middle-sized towns.

B *Turn into the possessive case:*

1 the house of my brother.
2 the life of Keats
3 the car of the Burts.
4 the book of the friend of my aunt.
5 It represents the work of a week.
6 This is the crown of the Queen of England.
7 This is the house of Peter and Jane.
8 He made a speech of two hours.
9 We spent the week-end at the house of my uncle.
10 I must go to the shop of the hairdresser.
11 I didn't approve of the policies of Kennedy, Johnson and Nixon.

Pronoms personnels

Sujets	I	we	Compléments	me	us
	you	you		you	you
	he			him	
	she	they		her	them
	it			it	

Possessifs

Adjectifs	my	our	Pronoms	mine	ours
	your	your		yours	yours
	his			his	
	her	their		hers	theirs
	its			its	

Pronoms réfléchis et réciproques

1 / Réfléchis :   myself   ourselves
                  yourself   yourselves
                  himself
                  herself } themselves
                  itself

2 / Réciproques :   each other, one another

Noter la différence entre :

— The girls were looking at themselves in the mirror.

Les jeunes filles se regardaient (elles-mêmes) dans la glace.

— The girls were looking at each other and admiring each other.

Les jeunes filles se regardaient et s'admiraient (l'une l'autre, ou les unes les autres).

THE AFFLUENT SOCIETY

A *Use the proper possessive adjective or possessive pronoun or personal pronoun in the following sentences, as in the example:*

   Ex. : — She was looking at (he), at (he) funny face.
   →   — She was looking at <u>him</u>, at <u>his</u> funny face.

1 While I was talking to (she), she didn't listen to (I).
2 Peter said this was not (he) book; it is not (I) either, is it (you)?
3 The Morgans said they would call with (they) children, but I don't think I can stand being with (they) during the whole afternoon.
4 Why didn't you tell (I) you wanted (I) to talk to her?
5 "Is that (you) room?"
  "Yes, and the other one is (you)."
6 She insisted that it was (she) seat, (she) and nobody else's.
7 "Whose room is this?"   "(I), and nobody is to enter it."
8 "Is that (they) car?"   "No, it's not (they); it's (we)."
9 Don't look at (we) in this bewildered manner!
10 Look at the dog: isn't it pleased to see (it) master?

B *Use EACH OTHER / ONE ANOTHER or the proper reflexive pronoun:*

1 The two boxers were looking at ... before the round.
2 After the last round, he looked at ... and saw the extent of the damage.
3 You vain girl, stop looking at ... in the mirror!
4 Unable to answer the teacher's question, we were looking at ..., trying to avoid the teacher's eyes.
5 I hope you enjoyed ... on the trip.
6 We did enjoy ... though we didn't play with ... .
7 Help ... to some tea.
8 I think she wants to do this ... .
9 Stop quarrelling with ... .
10 Behave ..., you naughty boy!

Adjectif + gérondif

Le gérondif, qui est un nom verbal, peut être précédé d'un adjectif possessif. Il correspond alors au français « le fait que... »
Il peut être **sujet** :

— **Her being** so ill-bred always embarrasses her husband.

Le fait qu'elle soit si mal élevée cause toujours beaucoup de gêne à son mari.

ou **complément** :

— Do you mind **my smoking**?

Cela vous gêne-t-il que je fume?

Since = puisque

Since, conjonction, signifie 1) « depuis que ».
                                   2) « puisque » et exprime la cause.

Comparer :

— **Since** he failed in the entrance examination, he couldn't enter the business school.

Puisqu'il a raté l'examen d'admission, il n'a pas pu entrer dans cette école de préparation aux affaires.

— We haven't seen him **since** (the day when) he failed in his exam.

Nous ne l'avons pas vu depuis qu'il a raté son examen.

A *Reword the sentences as in the example:*

Ex.: — The fact that he will come annoys me.
→   — His coming annoys me.

1 I am shocked by the fact he shows so much hypocrisy.
2 Do you mind the fact that she stays so late?
3 The fact that we went bankrupt surprised everybody.
4 The fact that you gamble so recklessly will cause your ruin.
5 The fact that he mentioned the technological gap between our countries was considered as a blunder.
6 I'm sure they were annoyed by the fact that he arrived so late.
7 The fact that they got married so early was rather unexpected.
8 I was not surprised at the fact that she said so.
9 She doesn't approve of the fact that he smokes so much.
10 Have you heard of the fact that they're going to the States?

B *Underline since when it expresses cause in the following sentences:*

1 Since her husband died she has never been seen to smile.
2 Since her husband was dead and she had to support her children, she took a job as a typist.
3 Since you are so clever, tell me how to get rid of them!
4 Since he doesn't want to help me, I'll do it myself.
5 I haven't been to Los Angeles since we went there together, but I wish we went again.
6 Since you knew those brokers well, why didn't you ask them to give you a "tip"?
7 Since the parts of our various models are similar we can use them in any of the models we build.
8 Since 1970, the year when we standardized our production, our profits have kept increasing steadily.
9 Since he lost his job he has not been the same man.
10 Since he couldn't find a job, his family had to live on the dole.

Traductions de la construction française « en + participe présent »

Cette construction sera rendue en anglais de manière différente selon l'idée qu'elle exprime.

1 / EN + PP exprime le **moyen** → **BY + PP**
— *Il gagne sa vie en écrivant des romans policiers.*

He makes a living **by** writing detective novels.

2 / EN + PP exprime une réaction de **surprise** ou de **peur** → **AT + PP** :
— *Les enfants eurent peur en voyant le taureau dans le champ.*

The children were frightened **at** seeing the bull in the field.

3 / La subordonnée décrit une action immédiatement antérieure à celle exprimée par la principale → **ON + PP** :
— *En sortant de l'école elle vit la voiture de son père.*

On going out of school she saw her father's car.

4 / Les deux actions exprimées par la principale et par la subordonnée sont simultanées.
a / on n'insiste pas sur la durée de l'action → **PP simple** :
— *Elle se promenait dans Bond Street en regardant les vitrines.*

She was walking in Bond Street, looking at the shopwindows.

b / on insiste sur la durée de l'action → **WHILE + PP** :
— *La ménagère tricotait tout en regardant la télévision.*

The housewife was knitting **while** watching television.

5 / Une des deux actions est comprise dans l'autre → **IN + PP** (in = in the process of) :
— *En traversant la rue, il s'est fait renverser par une voiture.*

In crossing the street he was run over by a car.

6 / **EN + PP** indique la **manière** dont une action est, a été ou sera réalisée → l'équivalent anglais est généralement une construction « sujet + verbe exprimant la manière + postposition ou préposition suivie d'un complément :
— *Il traversa la rue en courant.*

He ran across the street.

A *Complete the following sentences with by, at, on, while, if necessary:*

1 ... waiting for John and Mary, I listened to the news on the radio.
2 I was both pleased and surprised ... hearing that some young American executives now question the Work Ethic.
3 He has improved his position ... working hard all his life.
4 ... driving back home he saw a dreadful accident on the road.
5 There is no doubt that it was ... hearing that he was bankrupt that he had a stroke.
6 They managed to make the workers work overtime ... promising them higher wages.
7 She was putting away some files, ... paying no attention to what was going on around her.
8 ... carrying on research for his own account, he has a part-time job with an industrial firm.
9 I wonder how he can bear to work on the assembly-line all day, ... deriving no pleasure from his work and ... never being able to leave his station.
10 It was ... striking repeatedly that they finally obtained what they wanted.
11 ... seeing that their demands were not met, they got furious.
12 They went away, ... airing their grievances and ... expressing their bitterness.
13 It was ... repairing the roof that he fell from a ladder.
14 ... taking such a measure you are sure to make the workers furious.
15 ... realizing that he had been cheated he flew into a rage.
16 ... walking to the office I met my secretary.
17 She was bewildered ... hearing that her little boy had been so rude.
18 I understood that there was something wrong ... entering the workshop.
19 The children were playing in the yard, ... shouting and ... laughing.
20 ... seeing him turn pale I realized how tired he was.

Indéfinis

a/ s'emploient avec un nom singulier :
MUCH (phrases négatives) et **A LOT OF** (phrases affirmatives) = beaucoup de :
- He doesn't earn **much** money.
- He earns **a lot of** money.

MANY A = maintes :
- *Il nous a averti maint(es) fois.*

  He warned us **many a** time.

LITTLE = peu de :
- *Il a peu de chance.*

  He has **little** luck.

A LITTLE = un peu de :
- *Il a gagné un peu d'argent.*

  He earned **a little** money.

b/ s'emploient avec un nom pluriel :
MANY = beaucoup de :
- *Ils ont beaucoup de livres.*

  They have **many** books.

FEW = peu de :
- *Ils ont peu d'amis.*

  They have **few** friends.

A FEW = quelques :
- *Vous avez fait quelques fautes.*

  You made **a few** mistakes.

SEVERAL = plusieurs :
- *Ils avaient invité plusieurs amis à leur soirée.*

  They had invited **several** friends to their party.

c/ s'emploient avec un nom singulier ou pluriel :
A LOT OF = **PLENTY OF** : beaucoup de.

THE AFFLUENT SOCIETY

A *Use MUCH or MANY in the following sentences:*

1 You needn't put so ... water on your plants.
2 ... big firms open up branches abroad.
3 I don't have as ... free time as you have.
4 There are ... banks and corporations which have their head-offices in Wall Street.
5 ... industries have their own laboratories.

B *Turn the sentences into the negative form as in the example:*

Ex.: a/ They have less money than we have.
→ b/ They don't have as much money as we have.
or : a/ They have fewer friends than we have.
→ b/ They don't have as many friends as we have.

1 There are fewer self-made men in Europe than in the U.S.
2 There is less staff in their company than in ours.
3 Mr Smith has less influence on the workers than the other foremen.
4 They have sold fewer shares than yesterday.
5 They employ fewer scientists than we do in our laboratory.
6 There are fewer workers on strike than last time.

C *Use LITTLE or FEW in the following sentences:*

1 With ... work and ... luck, you are bound to fail.
2 He has too ... friends to expect any help.
3 This company has too ... power to be dangerous for us.
4 There is too ... time left for the work to be finished in time.
5 So ... of the workers went on strike that they couldn't expect their claims to be met.

Test

1 I was extremely interested in ... he said.
- a/ this
- b/ what
- c/ which
- d/ that

2 Many Americans tend to believe that the unemployed are lazy people, ... to me seems most unfair.
- a/ this
- b/ what
- c/ which
- d/ that

3 Which of the following sentences is <u>wrong</u>?
- a/ This is the American conception of the Work Ethic
- b/ This is the American's conception of the Work Ethic
- c/ This is the Americans' conception of the Work Ethic
- d/ This is the Americans's conception of the Work Ethic

4 Do you know whether ... business is doing well?
- a/ Mr Jones
- b/ Mr Jones'
- c/ Mr Jones's
- d/ Mr Joneses'

5 Didn't you know this was ... room, not ... or ....
- a/ mine / yours / their
- b/ my / your / their
- c/ my / your / theirs
- d/ my / yours / theirs

6 This flat belongs to us: it is ....
- a/ our
- b/ us
- c/ ours
- d/ the our

7 The two little girls were talking ... in their baby's prattle.
- a/ each other
- b/ to each other
- c/ themselves
- d/ one another

8 Aren't you surprised ...?
- a/ that he succeeds so well
- b/ by his succeeding so well
- c/ by Peter' succeeding so well
- d/ what he succeeds so well

THE AFFLUENT SOCIETY 99

9 "It was no use trying to convince him ... he was determined to do as he pleased."
- a/ for
- b/ since
- c/ as
- d/ else

Which of these solutions is not correct?

10 He has not called on us ever ... he settled down in the neighbourhood.
- a/ since
- b/ for
- c/ ago
- d/ as

11 Peter can work ... listening to the radio.
- a/ as
- b/ while
- c/ on
- d/ —

12 ... speculating on the Stock Exchange he has made a fortune.
- a/ On
- b/ For
- c/ —
- d/ By

13 He had not foreseen a strike and was surprised ... hearing that the workers had not resumed work on Monday morning.
- a/ at
- b/ on
- c/ by
- d/ while

14 I heard the news ... getting in New York.
- a/ at
- b/ on
- c/ by
- d/ while

15 For ... Americans earning ... money is moral.
- a/ many / few
- b/ many / a lot of
- c/ much / little
- d/ few / many

16 He works as ... willingly as I do.
- a/ many
- b/ much
- c/ few
- d/ —

17 ... people are now conscious of the shortcomings of the Work Ethic.
- a/ Many
- b/ Much
- c/ Little
- d/ A little

18 Thanks to business combinations, ... firms can control one branch of industry.
- a/ many a
- b/ much
- c/ a little
- d/ a few

19 He is ... proud of being a self-made man.
- a/ many
- b/ a little
- c/ a few
- d/ few

20 He has as ... luck as I have, and even ... friends.
- a/ few / few
- b/ much / few
- c/ little / fewer
- d/ many / many

THE AFFLUENT SOCIETY

A *Translate into English :*

1 Selon certains sociologues, ce qui a favorisé le développement du capitalisme, c'est le protestantisme.
2 Il pense que le travail est un devoir religieux, ce qui est une attitude assez répandue.
3 Les Américains vénèrent l'éthique du travail, ce qui explique la remarquable vitalité de ce pays.
4 Ce que vous avancez est fort intéressant, mais avec quels arguments étayez-vous vos théories?
5 Ce que certains considèrent comme l'État Providence, d'autres le voient comme un encouragement à la paresse.
6 Ce que cet administrateur vient de suggérer pourrait mettre en danger toute notre politique.
7 Il croit à la libre entreprise, ce qui est son droit; je crois à l'intervention du gouvernement, ce qui est mon droit à moi.
8 Nous allons ouvrir une filiale dans ce pays, ce qui nous permettra de nous emparer du marché.
9 Ce qui nous permettra de nous emparer du marché, c'est l'absence totale d'industries locales.
10 Les lois anti-trusts ne sont pas toujours appliquées, ce qui est fort regrettable.

B *Translate into English :*

1 C'est ma voiture, ce n'est pas celle de John, ce n'est pas la vôtre, c'est la mienne et celle de personne d'autre!
2 Voici votre maison, voici la nôtre, voici celle des Wilson, et là-bas se trouve celle des Jones.
3 « Vous êtes sûr que c'est le sac de Joan? »
« Puisque ce n'est ni le vôtre, ni le mien, ce ne peut être que le sien. »
4 Peter a amené un chien; il a dit que ce n'était pas le sien. Puisque ce n'est pas le vôtre ni celui de nos voisins, nous allons le garder ici.
5 Regardez Mr and Mrs Wilson dans leur nouvelle voiture; ils disent que c'est la leur, mais je crois qu'ils l'ont empruntée.

C *Translate into English:*

1 Ces deux sociétés ne cessent de rivaliser.
2 Ils se sont disputés pendant deux heures avant d'arriver à un accord.
3 Amusez-vous bien pendant que vous êtes jeunes.
4 Il s'aime et je m'adore : nous nous entendons fort bien.
5 Cessez de vous parler, s'il vous plaît.

D *Translate into English:*

1 Le fait qu'il nous ait aidés était plutôt inattendu.
2 Je n'approuve pas du tout le fait qu'elle fume tant.
3 Le fait qu'ils nous aient rendu visite a été une surprise fort agréable.
4 Je suis très déçu par le fait qu'il ait épousé une fille aussi ennuyeuse.
5 N'êtes-vous pas étonné par le fait qu'elle se rende à cette manifestation ?

E *Translate into English:*

1 En rentrant à la maison, j'ai vu que les enfants n'étaient pas revenus.
2 La petite fille rentra chez elle en pleurant parce qu'elle n'aimait pas l'école.
3 Miss Smith gagne sa vie en donnant des leçons d'anglais.
4 J'écoutais la radio en lisant le journal.
5 Je suis surprise de voir qu'il n'a pas suivi mes conseils.
6 En me rendant à Londres par avion, j'ai fait la connaissance de ce charmant vieux monsieur.

F *Translate into English:*

1 Elle a traversé la rivière à la nage.
2 Nous avons descendu les escaliers en courant.
3 Il a monté l'escalier en boitant.
4 Elles sont passées devant la maison à cheval.
5 Ils sont sortis du port en bateau.

1 Poverty and unemployment

For all its achievements, the affluent society has neglected many of its citizens who live in straitened circumstances.

1 Who is poor in America?
The Blacks have always represented and still represent the bulk of the American poor.
To them must be added the illegal immigrants (the Mexican "Wetbacks" for instance), the members of the ethnic minorities, many aged people, most unskilled workers, a number of small farmers and the unemployed.
This "other America" includes about 50 million citizens whose basic needs of food and shelter are still unsatisfied.

2 The living conditions of the poor
As many well-off Americans choose to live in the suburbs, the city centres are often left to the less privileged classes. Neglect and lack of money for repairs soon turn the shabby and shoddy buildings into decaying slums which become hotbeds of crime and violence.

In this land of plenty, rising food prices have sometimes led elderly and poor people to consume pet food which was all they could afford.

The children of the poor bear the brunt of an educational system organized on the local level. Besides, they have more opportunities of playing truant and thus the rate of school dropouts is high among the children of the underprivileged.

3 Unemployment
The poor are hit hardest by economic crises and their aftermaths.
When an industry reduces its production, many workers are laid off. They join the ranks of the jobless, which means registering at an unemployment agency and standing in a line for hours only to be told that there are no jobs available. To the material and moral dejection of the unemployed must be added the general lack of consideration towards the man who does not work. The Work Ethic is so deep-rooted in American minds that the unemployed tend to find fault with themselves rather than with a system whose values they still worship.

THE SEAMY SIDE OF THE AFFLUENT SOCIETY

for	malgré
an a**chieve**ment	une réalisation
in **strait**ened **circ**umstances	dans la gêne

1

the **bulk**	la masse
the "**Wet**backs" (1)	les "Wetbacks"
the **un**em**ployed**	les chômeurs
to in**clude**	comprendre
basic	fondamental
shelter	abri → logement

2

well-**off**	aisé
ne**glect**	mauvais entretien
re**pairs**	réparations
shabby	miteux
shoddy	de camelote
de**cay**ing	qui se délabre
slums	taudis
hotbeds	foyers
land of **plen**ty	terre d'abondance
rising **food pric**es	l'augmentation du prix des produits alimentaires
elderly	âgé
to con**sume**	consommer
pet food	nourriture pour chiens et chats
to af**ford**	avoir les moyens d'acheter
to **bear** the **brunt**	faire les frais
to **play tru**ant	faire l'école buissonnière

a **school drop**out	quelqu'un qui a interrompu ses études
the **un**der**pri**vileged	les défavorisés

3

to be **hit**	être frappé
aftermath(s)	suites
laid off	congédiés
the **job**less	les chômeurs
to **stand** in (a) **line**	faire la queue
a**vail**able	disponible
de**jec**tion	accablement
to **find fault** with	critiquer
to **wor**ship	adorer, vénérer

OTHER WORDS AND PHRASES

to **live** from **hand** to **mouth**	vivre au jour le jour
penniless = impe**cu**nious = **hard up**	sans le sou
to be **broke**	être fauché
unable to **make** both **ends meet**	incapable de joindre les deux bouts
poor as **Job**	pauvre comme Job
to **keep** the **wolf** from the **door**	parer à la misère
things go from **bad** to **worse**	les choses vont de mal en pis

---

1. Aussi appelés « mojados », les « Wetbacks » sont les immigrants mexicains qui ont parfois dû traverser le Rio Grande à la nage.

2 Rebellion

The <u>inequities</u> which exist in American society, the racial problems, the dehumanization of work and life by modern technology, and, above all, the Vietnam war, led many young Americans to reject the traditional values cherished by <u>their elders</u>.
This rebellion took place in the sixties. It was essentially a middle-class phenomenon.

1 "The Greening of America"
According to Charles A. Reich, who published *The Greening of America* in 1970, it was the young who, by their rebellion, <u>set off</u> a movement which might <u>ultimately</u> transform America. This revolt was to be found at <u>all</u> levels of society but, more than anywhere else, among the students. The numerous <u>sit-ins,</u> marches and <u>demonstrations</u> which then took place on university campuses <u>testified to</u> the vitality of the student movement.

2 The young rebels
It was not <u>merely</u> in their <u>speeches</u> and <u>arguments</u> that the young questioned the traditional values. Their <u>whole</u> behaviour, their long hair and their colourful clothes were all symbols of their protest.
Sometimes the rejection of the family and <u>social background</u> was so complete that they left home. They became <u>transients</u>, <u>hitch-hiking</u> their way to California, or hippies and lived in a commune. They would lead a life free from <u>the shackles</u> of convention, the life of <u>the "flower people"</u>. They begged when they felt the lack of money, and seemed <u>genuinely</u> interested in music, poetry and all forms of art.

3 The rebellion on the wane
In the 1970s the revolt of the young began <u>to abate</u>.
Many movements had been diluted by their own distaste for organization, and rebellion appeared more as a style of life than as a political credo.
However, it was with the American <u>withdrawal</u> from Vietnam that the <u>chief</u> cause of <u>unrest</u> disappeared.
Then the preoccupation with youth's rebellion was drowned in the general <u>tide</u> of anxiety caused by the economic <u>depression</u>.

THE SEAMY SIDE OF THE AFFLUENT SOCIETY

inequities	injustices
their **el**ders	leurs aînés

1

to **set off**	donner l'élan à
ultimately	en fin de compte
a **sit**-in	une occupation des lieux
a **de**monstration	une manifestation
to **test**ify to	témoigner de

2

merely	simplement, seulement
a **speech**	un discours
an **ar**gument	1 / une discussion 2 / un argument
whole	dans son ensemble
social **back**ground	milieu social
a **tran**sient	un voyageur
to **hitch**-hike	faire de l'auto-stop
the **shack**les	les entraves
the **flow**er **peo**ple	les hippies
genuinely	réellement

3

on the **wane**	sur le déclin
to a**bate**	se calmer
with**draw**al	retrait (des troupes)
chief (adj.)	principal(e)
unrest	agitation
tide	marée (ici : vague)
de**pres**sion	crise

OTHER WORDS AND PHRASES

---

the gene**ra**tion **gap**	le conflit des générations
a con**straint**	une contrainte
to **free** one**self**	se libérer
discon**tent**	le mécontentement
to de**nounce**	dénoncer
to **ad**vocate	préconiser
militancy	le militantisme
to **make** a **stand** a**gainst**	s'élever contre
draft (U.S.)	la conscription
to a**bo**lish	abolir
a consci**en**tious ob**jec**tor	un objecteur de conscience
an up**heav**al	un soulèvement
left-**wing** (adj.)	de gauche

3 Crime, violence and drugs

1 Crime and violence
Pilfering, shoplifting, purse-snatching are minor offences, but the number of hold-ups with the taking of hostages, rapes, and murders in American cities (New York and Chicago in particular) is staggering. More terrifying still are the crimes of the "Mousepacks", gangs of young boys who perpetrate the most cruel and gratuitous acts.

American city-dwellers have become used to taking precautions against thugs. They avoid going out at night, and when they have to, they keep their eyes open.

Armed guards, locked doors, and specially trained police patrols are not sufficient to deter criminals. The rising crime-rate causes a general feeling of insecurity.

2 Drugs
It is significant that crime often follows on the heels of the drug problem. They are closely linked: they often have the same roots, were often bred by the same unsatisfactory conditions or the same disillusionments.

There is a big gap between the youth who occasionally smokes "grass" or other non-addictive drugs and the inveterate drug-addict prepared to do anything to obtain a "fix". But who knows what a shrewd "pusher" will do to induce a weak youth to become a regular drug-user, to turn him from a "straight" into a "head"?

3 The fight against drug-usage
To deter the young from using drugs, the Americans have turned to education. Young people are warned of the dangers of drug-addiction: irreparable harm done to the grey cells of the brain and to the chromosomes.

More important are the measures taken against the smugglers and traffickers who incur serious sentences, or the dismantling of such networks as the "French connection".

However, many people point out that the prime aim of the fight against drugs should be the eradication of poverty, of unemployment and racism which are, according to them, the fundamental causes of this plague.

THE SEAMY SIDE OF THE AFFLUENT SOCIETY

1

pilfering	larcins
shoplifting	vol à l'étalage
purse-snatching	vol à la tire
minor of**fen**ces	petits délits
a **hos**tage	un otage
a **rape**	un viol
staggering	atterrant
more ... still	encore plus
to **per**petrate	commettre, perpétrer (un crime)
a **ci**ty-dweller	un citadin
a **thug** (slang)	un agresseur
to de**ter**	pour décourager
rising	en augmentation

2

sig**ni**ficant	significatif
on the **heels**	sur les talons
linked	lié(s)
a **root**	une racine
bred ← to **breed**	engendrer
a **gap**	un fossé
oc**ca**sionally	à l'occasion
"**grass**"	« l'herbe », la marijuana
non-ad**dic**tive	qui ne produit pas d'accoutumance
in**ve**terate	invétéré
a **drug-ad**dict	un drogué
a "**fix**"	une injection de drogue
shrewd	rusé, habile
a "**push**er"	celui qui entraîne à prendre de la drogue
to in**duce**	pousser à
a "**straight**"	celui qui ne se drogue pas (1)
a "**head**"	celui qui se drogue (1)

3

to **warn**	avertir
harm	tort, mal
the **grey cells**	les cellules grises
a **smug**gler	un contrebandier
a **traf**ficker	un trafiquant
to in**cur** a **sen**tence	encourir une condamnation
dis**mant**ling	démantèlement
a **net**work	un réseau
prime	le plus important
eradi**ca**tion	suppression totale
a **plague**	un fléau

OTHER WORDS AND PHRASES

a **mug**ger (slang)	un agresseur
hard drugs = ad**dic**tive **drugs**	drogues qui créent une accoutumance
a **joint**	un joint
pot	la marijuana
to **take** "a **trip**"	« faire un voyage » (se droguer)

---

1. Argot des étudiants.

4 The colour problem

Though all ethnic minorities suffer from discrimination, no group has been as sorely tried as the Blacks.

1 Slavery and the roots of racism

In the days of slavery, some Blacks had already rebelled against their white masters (Nat Turner's revolt for instance). Others fled to the North or even to Canada, with the help of the "underground railroad", a clandestine organization.

At the end of the Civil War, all attempts to reconstruct a mixed society were checked by the activities of the Ku Klux Klan and the general hostility of the Whites.

The doctrine of "separate but equal" finally prevailed. In fact it meant the acceptance of discrimination and of an inferior status for the Blacks.

2 The fight against discrimination

The XXth century has witnessed the creation of associations whose aim is the actual integration of the Blacks.

In 1964, the *Civil Rights Act* gave the Blacks equal rights, theoretically at least. But integration has not yet been achieved in fact.

The riots and protests caused by busing (i.e. the transporting of Black children to White schools and of White children to schools located in Black districts) leave little room for hope. This and other similar failures may explain why some Black nationalist movements prefer to demand the creation of a separate Negro nation within the borders of the U.S.

3 Today's Black America

In spite of the measures taken, racism still prevails in the U.S.

To the racial problem is added a social problem. Because they often receive a mediocre education and because they are discriminated against, the Blacks are always given the most menial and least paid jobs. Most of them remain in the low-income brackets and have no hope of ever improving their social status. Moreover, they are always more affected than the Whites by economic difficulties (the unemployment rate is four times as high among the Blacks as among the Whites). It is therefore not surprising that their reactions against a society which has thus ill-used them should at times be violent.

THE SEAMY SIDE OF THE AFFLUENT SOCIETY

as **sore**ly **tried** as	aussi éprouvé que

1

al**rea**dy	déjà
to **flee, fled, fled**	fuir
the "**un**derground **rail**road" (1)	le « chemin de fer souterrain »
an at**tempt**	une tentative
to **check**	tenir en échec
to pre**vail**	1 / l'emporter 2 / régner, prédominer

2

to **wit**ness	être le témoin de
actual	réel
a **ri**ot	une émeute
leave little **room** for **hope**	laissent peu d'espoir
a **fail**ure	un échec
to de**mand**	exiger
with**in** the **bor**ders	à l'intérieur des frontières

3

menial	servile, désagréable
the **low-in**come **brack**ets	les tranches de salaires les plus basses
social **sta**tus	position sociale
four times as **high** ... as	quatre fois plus élevé ... que
to **ill-use**	traiter mal
at **times**	parfois

OTHER WORDS AND PHRASES

a **Ne**gro	un Noir
a **nig**ger	un nègre (péjoratif)
a **whi**tey = a **Char**ley = a **hon**ky	un blanc (péjoratif)

H.O.M.E. = **Home** Opportunities **Made** **E**qual (2)

a **pre**judice	un préjugé
narrow-mindedness	étroitesse d'esprit
bitterness	amertume (sens propre et figuré)
con**tempt**	mépris
hatred	haine

Organisations antiracistes

N.A.A.C.P. = **Na**tional Associa**ti**on for the Ad**vance**ment of **Col**ored **Peo**ple

S.C.L.C. = **Sou**thern **Chris**tian **Lea**dership **Con**ference

C.O.R.E. = **Con**gress of **Ra**cial E**qual**ity

S.N.C.C. ("snick") = **Stu**dent **Non**violent **Co**ordinating Com**mit**tee

---

1. La filière clandestine qui organisait la fuite des esclaves noirs du Sud vers les États non-esclavagistes du Nord.
2. Organisation ayant pour but d'introduire des familles noires dans des quartiers blancs.

Grammar and exercises

Comparatif et superlatif

Comparatifs et superlatifs de supériorité :

1/ Adj. courts : small → small**er** than → **the** small**est**

2/ Adj. longs : beautiful → **more** beautiful **than**
→ **the most** beautiful.

3/ Adj. de deux syllabes terminés par **y, er, le** :
        happy → happ**ier** → **the** happ**iest**
        clever → { clever**er** → **the** clever**est**
                  { **more** clever → **the most** clever

4/ Comparatifs et superlatifs irréguliers :
    good, well → better than → the best
    bad, ill → worse than → the worst
    far → farther than → the farthest (distance)
           further than → the furthest (idées, temps) (1)
    old → older than → the oldest
          elder (épithète non suivi de **than** pour frères
          et sœurs) → the eldest
    late → later → the latest (le plus récent)
           latter → the last (le dernier)

Comparatif d'égalité :
    as + **adj.** + **as** → He is as rich as you (are).

Comparatif d'inégalité
    not so + **adj.** + **as** → He is not so rich as you (are).

Comparatif et superlatif d'infériorité :
    less + **adj.** + **than** → He is less rich than you (are).
    the least + **adj.** → He is the least intelligent
                      person I've ever met.

Équivalent du français « d'autant plus que » :
— *Je suis d'autant plus contrarié que je ne m'y attendais pas.*

I'm **(all) the more upset as** I didn't expect it.

---

1. Cette deuxième forme l'emporte maintenant la première tend à disparaître.

THE SEAMY SIDE OF THE AFFLUENT SOCIETY

A *Complete the following sentences using the adjective in brackets in the superlative:*

1 (demanding)   He is ... person I've ever met.
2 (good)   This is ... play I've ever seen.
3 (bad)   He is ... leader we could choose.
4 (late)   This is ... news from London.
5 (late)   I'm reading ... chapter of this book.
6 (bad-looking)   He is ... chap I've ever seen.
7 (well-dressed)   She is ... woman I know.
8 (old)   We have 3 children: John is ... .

B *Reword the following sentences as in the example:*
    Ex.: a/ He is rich; so are you.
    → b/ You are as rich as he is.

1 Peter is young; so am I.
2 They are destitute; so are we.
3 The Smiths are penniless; so are you.
4 Their house is decrepit; so is ours.
5 Pushers are dangerous; so are traffickers.

C *Reword the following sentences as in the example:*
    Ex.: a/ He is less active than his wife.
    → b/ He is not so active as his wife.

1 Their house is less pleasant than ours.
2 Your children are less rebellious than the Joneses'.
3 Mary is less plain than her elder sister.
4 Your living conditions are less bad than those of your Black fellow-workers.
5 The wages of the Blacks are less high than those of Whites in similar jobs.

Progression exprimée par la répétition du comparatif

- The case is **more and more** serious.
  L'affaire est de plus en plus *grave*.

- She is getting weak**er and** weak**er.**
  Elle est de plus en plus *faible*.

- TV programs are **less and less** interesting.
  Les programmes de télévision sont de moins en moins *intéressants*.

Progression parallèle exprimée par le comparatif

- **The older** he gets, **the less** wise he becomes.
  Plus *il vieillit,* moins *il est sage.*

- **The more** he works, **the happier** he looks.
  Plus *il travaille,* plus *il a l'air heureux.*

Traduction de « faire + infinitif »

1/ Le complément est passif → **to have** + complément
  + participe passé :
  – *J'ai fait construire une maison.*

  I've had a house built.

2/ Le complément est actif → **to make** + complément
  + **infinitif sans to** :
  – *Le professeur fait travailler ses élèves.*

  The teacher makes his pupils work.

THE SEAMY SIDE OF THE AFFLUENT SOCIETY

A *Complete the sentences, using a double comparative in order to express progression, as in the example:*
   Ex.: — (expensive) Food is ...
   → — Food is more and more expensive

1 (high)   Prices are ...
2 (late)   The children go to bed ...
3 (bad)   My health is ...
4 (popular)   This leader is ...
5 (far)   Holiday-makers have to go ... to find unspoilt beaches.
6 (destitute) Owing to the crisis the poor are ...

B *Express parallel progression as in the example:*
   Ex.: — (popular, rich) ... he grows, ... this singer is.
   → — The more popular he grows, the richer this singer is.

1 (well, little)   ... I know him, ... I like him.
2 (well, nice)   ... acquainted we get, ... I find her.
3 (soon, happy)   ... you come, ... we'll be.
4 (bad)   The more he drinks, ... he looks.
5 (far)   ... you go, the more things you'll see.
6 (old, well-off)   ... we get, ... we are.

C *Reword the sentence as in the example:*
   Ex.: a/ Under her influence I work better.
   → b/ She makes me work better.

1 Because of the inequities they see in their society, some young Americans rebel.
2 Under the influence of despair he committed a robbery.
3 Because of his drug-addiction, he became a criminal.
4 Under the influence of a pusher he became a drug-addict.
5 Thanks to the arrival of the police patrol, the mugger fled.
6 Under your influence I find life more pleasant.

Used to

Deux constructions possibles qui ne doivent pas être confondues :

1/ — I'm **used to working** hard.
   — J'ai (maintenant) l'habitude de travailler beaucoup.

2/ — I **used to play** tennis when I was young.
   — Je jouais au tennis quand j'étais jeune.

La première construction exprime une habitude actuelle (présent), la deuxième est la forme fréquentative qui exprime une habitude passée.

But et conséquence exprimés par « for »

1/ Idée de but :
   — I've made this tea **for you to drink.**
   J'ai fait ce thé pour que tu le boives.

2/ Idée de conséquence :
   — This house is too old **for us to live** in it.
   Cette maison est trop vieille pour que nous y vivions.

Composés de « ever »

Who, what, which, when, where, how peuvent tous former un composé avec **ever** pour exprimer l'éventualité, l'incertitude :

— **Wherever** he may go, they'll find him.
   Où qu'il aille, ils le trouveront.

— **Whoever** said that spoke the truth.
   Quelle que soit la personne qui a dit cela, elle a dit la vérité.

THE SEAMY SIDE OF THE AFFLUENT SOCIETY

A *Complete the sentences with <u>used to + verb</u> in correct form:*

1 The poor (to live) in decaying slums.
2 When we were young we (to live) in the country.
3 The Negroes (to be) ill-treated by the Whites.
4 When he was a child his parents (to ill-treat) him.
5 When we were just married we (to be) unable to make ends meet.
6 The American city-dwellers (to lock) their doors.
7 When I was a student I (to denounce) the system.
8 Now I (to live) in it.

B *Reword the sentences as in the example:*
  Ex.: — Their prices are too high; we can't buy from them.
    → — Their prices are too high for us to buy from them.

1 The room is too noisy; I can't work in peace.
2 Those prejudices are too deep-rooted; we can't eradicate them.
3 The American Whites are too prejudiced; desegregation can't be achieved.
4 The gangsters proved too shrewd; the police couldn't arrest them.
5 He is too inveterate a drug-addict; the doctor can't save him.
6 The car went too fast; I couldn't see the faces of the people inside.

C *Use the proper "ever"-form in the following sentences:*

1 Tell the children they're not supposed to do ... they feel like doing.
2 They said they'd come ... they could.
3 ... said that was a fool.
4 Take ... of my books you want.
5 ... you go, you find too many tourists in Summer.
6 I met Jones, or Jounes, or ... his name is.

Test

(Ce test ne comporte que 18 questions.)

1 John has three brothers but he is ....
- □ a/ the older
- □ b/ the elder
- □ c/ older
- □ d/ the eldest

2 We are not very rich and they are ... than we are.
- □ a/ not so well-off
- □ b/ as well-off
- □ c/ better-off
- □ d/ well-off

3 Jane is ... Mary.
- □ a/ not so clever as
- □ b/ so clever as
- □ c/ so clever than
- □ d/ not so clever than

4 Mr Jones and Mr Smith are both friends of mine, but I like ... better.
- □ a/ the later
- □ b/ the last
- □ c/ the latter
- □ d/ later

5 They are very disappointed, ... they expected to improve their position.
- □ a/ the most as
- □ b/ the more so as
- □ c/ more so as
- □ d/ the more so than

6 They are ... they had hoped to change their society.
- □ a/ most disillusioned
- □ b/ the more disillusioned as
- □ c/ more disillusioned than
- □ d/ most disillusioned than

7 ... we work together, ... I appreciate him.
- □ a/ The more so/as
- □ b/ The more/the more
- □ c/ The most/the most
- □ d/ More/more

8 The music master ... by the pupils.
- □ a/ had a song sung
- □ b/ had a song sing
- □ c/ make a song sing
- □ d/ made a song sung

9
- □ a/ They had the whole firm reorganize
- □ b/ They made the whole firm reorganize
- □ c/ They made the whole firm reorganized
- □ d/ They had the whole firm reorganized

THE SEAMY SIDE OF THE AFFLUENT SOCIETY

10 The leader ... .
- [ ] a/ made them demonstrate
- [ ] b/ made them demonstrated
- [ ] c/ had them demonstrated
- [ ] d/ had them demonstrating

11 The unskilled workers ... insecurity.
- [ ] a/ used to
- [ ] b/ used to living in
- [ ] c/ are used to
- [ ] d/ are used to live in

12 When I was a child, my parents ... penniless by the 20th of the month.
- [ ] a/ are used to being
- [ ] b/ used to be
- [ ] c/ used to being
- [ ] d/ were used to be

13 ... I could, I ... truant.
- [ ] a/ However/am used to play
- [ ] b/ Whenever/was used to play
- [ ] c/ Whenever/used to play
- [ ] d/ However/am used to playing

14 American city-dwellers have become ... precautions against muggers.
- [ ] a/ used to take
- [ ] b/ are used to taking
- [ ] c/ used to have taken
- [ ] d/ used to taking

15 We bought this house ... in it.
- [ ] a/ for our children to live
- [ ] b/ that our children might live
- [ ] c/ in order that our children might live
- [ ] d/ for that our children live

Which of these solutions is not correct

16 This book is too uninteresting ... it.
- [ ] a/ for me to read
- [ ] b/ for I to read
- [ ] c/ for that I read it
- [ ] d/ for that I might read

17 I bought this book in order that ... my English.
- [ ] a/ I improve
- [ ] b/ I'll improve
- [ ] c/ I might improve
- [ ] d/ I must improve

18 ... young he may be, he has no excuse for acting in such a disgraceful manner.
- [ ] a/ However
- [ ] b/ Whatever
- [ ] c/ Whenever
- [ ] d/ Whichever

A *Translate into English:*

1 Je trouve leur situation aussi intéressante que la vôtre.
2 Les enfants des pauvres Blancs ne sont pas tout à fait aussi malheureux que les enfants des pauvres Noirs.
3 Ils ne sont pas aussi politiquement actifs que nous.
4 La révolte des jeunes Américains n'est pas aussi violente qu'auparavant.
5 C'est l'homme le moins actif que je connaisse.
6 Il est d'autant plus malheureux qu'il est maintenant au chômage.
7 Il est très malheureux, d'autant plus qu'il est maintenant au chômage.
8 Ils sont d'autant plus pauvres qu'ils ont été touchés par la crise.
9 Le salaire de ces ouvriers est d'autant plus bas que ce sont des immigrants clandestins.
10 Il est d'autant moins excusable qu'il appartient à une classe privilégiée.
11 Les gens qui remettent en cause l'éthique du travail sont de plus en plus nombreux.
12 Plus il y en a, mieux c'est.
13 Les drogués sont malheureusement de plus en plus nombreux.
14 Moins il y en a, mieux c'est.
15 Plus leurs parents sont pauvres, moins ils ont de chances de faire des études.

B *Translate into English:*

1 Je me suis fait couper les cheveux.
2 Nous avons fait aider les personnes âgées.
3 Faites-le venir à mon bureau.
4 C'est lui qui m'a fait prendre de la drogue pour la première fois.
5 Ils font attendre les chômeurs pendant des heures.
6 Nos voisins ont fait réparer leur vieille maison délabrée.
7 Le retrait américain du Vietnam a fait se calmer quelque peu la révolte des étudiants.

THE SEAMY SIDE OF THE AFFLUENT SOCIETY

C *Translate into English:*

1 Ils ont l'habitude de manifester quand ils ne sont pas contents.
2 Les Noirs sont habitués à vivre dans des taudis délabrés.
3 Quand il était petit, il traînait dans les rues toute la journée.
4 Les travailleurs non qualifiés sont habitués à recevoir des salaires ridiculement bas.
5 Les citadins sont maintenant habitués à être témoins de hold-ups aux États-Unis.
6 Ils habitaient des quartiers résidentiels quand ils étaient jeunes.

D *Translate into English (using "for"):*

1 Il est trop vieux maintenant pour que je lui trouve un emploi.
2 Le quartier est trop pauvre pour que l'on améliore les écoles.
3 Ils sont trop nombreux pour que nous puissions les vaincre.
4 Ce criminel est trop endurci pour que nous espérions le sauver.
5 Cette école est trop médiocre pour que nos enfants y aillent.
6 Cette cravate est trop laide pour que vous la portiez ce soir.
7 Il y a trop de vols dans la ville pour que les habitants se sentent en sécurité le soir.
8 Il est trop tard pour qu'elle rentre seule à pied chez elle.

E *Translate into English:*

1 Où que vous alliez, quoi que vous fassiez, vous ne pouvez pas éviter ces gens.
2 Aussi nombreux que vous soyez, vous serez les bienvenus.
3 Quelle que soit la personne qui a fait cela, elle mérite une récompense.
4 Prenez n'importe lequel de ces livres s'ils vous intéressent.
5 Venez quand vous voudrez.
6 Aussi jeune qu'il soit, il n'a aucune excuse pour s'être conduit ainsi.

1 The United States and World War II

Though it gave Great Britain and the Allied forces practically unlimited military aid under the Lend-Lease Act, the U.S. did not enter the war until December 1941.

1 The Japanese attack

Ever since 1937, Japan had made repeated attempts to crush China and to establish its authority over the whole of Eastern Asia.

After the Japanese had invaded Indochina in 1941, Roosevelt demanded that they should withdraw their troops from the French colony.

On December 7, 1941, the Japanese air force made a bold attack on Pearl Harbor where the U.S. Pacific fleet was anchored. The fleet was completely destroyed.

By the end of 1942, the Japanese occupied the Philippines, Burma, Hong Kong, Singapore and Indonesia.

2 The war in the Pacific

From 1943 on, the Americans began to strike back. They progressed slowly but steadily, winning back island after island. After massive air raids, the marines would storm the position. In the South, under the command of General MacArthur, most of the Philippines was reconquered by the beginning of 1945. When Iwoshima and Okinawa had been won back in the North, under the command of Admiral Nimitz, Tokyo was within reach of the U.S. superfortresses.

3 From the Battle of Normandy to the Japanese surrender

On June 6, 1944, under the command of General Eisenhower, the Allied forces disembarked on the shores of Normandy. Thus the Americans finally played an active part in a European war. So far, their role had been essentially to supply the Soviet Union and Great Britain with armaments. Meanwhile, however, the atomic bomb was being developed and completed. It was tested in New Mexico.

Landing troops in Japan would have cost the Americans over a million lives. Therefore President Truman ordered that the atomic bomb should be dropped on Hiroshima (Aug. 6, 1945) and Nagasaki (Aug. 9, 1945). On August 14, 1945, Japan capitulated. Twenty-one days had elapsed between the testing of the bomb and its use in warfare.

THE UNITED STATES IN THE WORLD

the **All**ied **for**ces	les Alliés
practically	à peu près
under the **Lend-Lease Act**	en vertu de la loi Prêt-Bail

1

Eastern **A**sia	l'Asie orientale
to with**draw troops**	retirer des troupes
bold	hardi
anchored	ancré
Burma	la Birmanie

2

From 1943 on	à partir de 1943
to **strike back**	répliquer (répondre aux coups)
to pro**gress**	avancer
steadily	régulièrement
to **win back**	reconquérir
to **storm** a po**si**tion	prendre une position d'assaut
wi**thin reach** of	à portée de
the **su**per**fort**resses	les forteresses volantes

3

sur**ren**der	capitulation
the **shores**	les côtes
to **play** a **part** = to **play** a **role**	jouer un rôle
so **far**	jusque-là
to sup**ply**	fournir
meanwhile	pendant ce temps
to com**plete**	terminer
to **land troops**	débarquer des troupes
to **cost, cost, cost**	coûter
over a **mil**lion **lives**	plus d'un million de vies
therefore	c'est pourquoi
to e**lapse**	s'écouler (temps)
warfare	la guerre

OTHER WORDS AND PHRASES

to de**clare** war u**pon**	déclarer la guerre à
to **check** an at**tack**	enrayer une attaque
a **wea**pon	une arme
bombing	bombardement
a **dug**-out	un abri
a **truce**	une trêve
a **peace**-settlement	un accord de paix
war casualties	les pertes (en hommes)
the **wound**ed	les blessés
nuclear **wea**pons	les armes nucléaires

2 The American leadership and the cold war

In spite of a common victory over Nazi Germany and the creation of the U.N. (United Nations), the opposition between the U.S. and the U.S.S.R. soon appeared. The cold war started in 1947.

1 The formation of two blocs (1947-1950)

With the Marshall Plan (1947-51), the U.S. showed the importance they attached to Europe and Latin America. By the creation of N.A.T.O., they reinforced their military influence over the Western world. Meanwhile, the Soviet Union organized Eastern Europe in a similar manner. The conflict over Berlin (1948-49) was the first crisis of the cold war.

After the explosion of the first Russian atomic bomb (1950), the U.S., under the influence of Senator McCarthy, was the scene of the persecution of people charged with having anti-American activities because of their left-wing opinions. This "witch-hunt" (1950-54) culminated in 1953 in the execution of the Rosenbergs.

2 Towards an open war?

The Korean War (1950-53) was officially conducted by the U.N. But, in fact, the American forces were its backbone.
There were fears that the Americans might use the atomic bomb and that the Russians might retaliate in Western Europe. Then there was the Indochina War (1950-54). Once the French had been defeated, the Americans took over the fight against communism in Vietnam.
In 1956, the events in Hungary showed that the U.S. were determined not to interfere within the boundaries of the Soviet bloc.

3 Towards pacific coexistence (1957-62)

In 1962, the Soviets made it known that they now had in their possession intercontinental rockets. They also launched the first Sputnik.
Other developments contributed to easing the relations between the two superpowers: the personality of Krutchev and the first frictions between China and the U.S.S.R., for instance. In spite of local conflicts, especially the Cuban crisis in 1962, this was the beginning of the era of pacific coexistence.

THE UNITED STATES IN THE WORLD

the U.N.	l'O.N.U.
the U.S.S.R. = the **U**nion of **So**viet **So**cialist Re**pu**blics	l'U.R.S.S.

1

a **bloc**	un bloc politique
N.A.T.O. = **N**orth **A**tlantic **T**reaty **O**rganiza**t**ion	l'O.T.A.N.
the **Wes**tern **W**orld	le monde occidental
Eastern	oriental(e)
similar	semblable
charged with **hav**ing	accusés d'avoir
left-wing	de gauche
the **witch**-hunt	la chasse aux sorcières (1)

2

to**wards**	vers
the Ko**re**an **War**	la guerre de Corée
con**duc**ted	menée
the A**me**rican **for**ces were its **back**bone	elle reposait sur les forces américaines
fears	craintes
to re**ta**liate	riposter
once	1 / une fois 2 / une fois que
to **take o**ver	reprendre
Hungary	la Hongrie
to inter**fere**	intervenir
wi**thin** the **boun**daries of	à l'intérieur des limites de

3

made it **known**	firent savoir
a **ro**cket	une fusée
to **launch**	lancer
to **ease** the re**la**tions	détendre les relations
the **two su**perpowers	les deux supergrands
era	ère

OTHER WORDS AND PHRASES

nuclear **ar**maments	armes nucléaires
S.A.L.T. = Stra**te**gic **Ar**mament Limi**ta**tion **Talks**	accords sur la limitation des armements stratégiques
techno**lo**gical **war**fare	la guerre scientifique
bio**lo**gical **war**fare	la guerre biologique
the **ba**lance of **po**wer	l'équilibre des forces
the **ba**lance of **ter**ror	l'équilibre de la terreur
the de**ter**rent **po**wer	la force de dissuasion
dé**tente**	la détente

---

1. Ainsi appelée parce que cette persécution rappelait celle exercée contre les « sorcières » dans les colonies d'Amérique au XVIIe siècle.

3 J. F. Kennedy: myth and reality

In 1960, Democrat J. F. Kennedy was elected President of the U.S. by a narrow majority.

1 The Kennedy myth

For the Americans, Kennedy is the man who caused the Soviet Union to yield in the Cuban missile crisis and the founder of the Alliance for Progress whose purpose is to aid Latin American peoples. Above all, he demonstrated the need for a "New Frontier", a change and improvement in American society. The "New Frontier" speech, Kennedy's Inaugural Address, set out the aims the President planned for his national policy: the necessity to abolish ignorance and prejudices, to solve the problems set by extreme wealth and extreme poverty, to develop scientific and space research.

The assassination of Kennedy in Dallas (November 1963) contributed to the myth of a statesman devoted to progress.

2 The facts

In actual fact, if we except space research, the failure of Kennedy's domestic policy is obvious.

All the plans for reform got bogged down in the quagmire of congressional debates. The F.B.I. remained extremely powerful and its interventions in political life continued as before. At the international level, the Bay of Pigs (1961) was a regrettable failure. Congress refused funds for the Alliance for Progress. A new armaments race with the Soviet Union started. Lastly, the Pentagon Papers have disclosed Kennedy's responsibility in the fatal American involvement in Vietnam.

3 The presidential myth on the wane

Though Lyndon B. Johnson had his own reform program, the Vietnam war detracted from all his efforts.

Richard Nixon pulled the U.S. out of Vietnam, but his popularity was wrecked by the Watergate scandal.

The series of scandals which followed Watergate (the disclosure of the interventions of the C.I.A. in the domestic policy of foreign countries with a view to stemming the spread of communism, the bribery of politicians by big corporations, etc...) have gradually tarnished the image the Americans had of their President, of their system and of themselves.

THE UNITED STATES IN THE WORLD 127

a **myth**	un mythe
by a **nar**row ma**jo**rity	à une faible majorité

1

to **yield**	céder
the **foun**der	le fondateur
the Alliance for **Pro**gress	l'Alliance pour le Progrès
a**bove** all	surtout
the In**au**gural Ad**dress**	le discours d'intronisation (1)
to **set out**	présenter, exposer
a **pre**judice	un préjugé (2)
space re**search**	la recherche spatiale
a **states**man	un homme d'État
de**vo**ted to	attaché à

2

in **ac**tual **fact**	en réalité
do**mes**tic **po**licy	la politique intérieure
obvious	évident
to **get bog**ged **down**	s'enliser
a **quag**mire	une fondrière
the F.B.I. = the **Fe**deral **Bu**reau of Investi**ga**tion	la police fédérale
the **Bay** of **Pigs**	la Baie des Cochons (3)
a **fail**ure	un échec
funds	fonds
ar**ma**ments **race**	course aux armements
lastly	enfin
to dis**close**	révéler
fatal	funeste
in**vol**vement	engagement

3

on the **wane**	sur le déclin
to de**tract** from	nuire à
was **wreck**ed	fut détruite
a **se**ries	une série
with a **view** to	dans le but de
to **stem**	endiguer, enrayer
the **spread**	l'expansion
bribery	corruption
a poli**ti**cian	un homme politique
to **tar**nish	ternir

---

1. **Inaugural Address**: discours prononcé par le Président américain le jour de son entrée en fonction **(Inauguration)**.
2. Faux-ami ! Cependant, **prejudice** peut signifier aussi « préjudice ».
3. Tentative d'invasion de Cuba par des exilés cubains, à l'instigation de la C.I.A., avec l'appui du gouvernement américain.

4 The Vietnam War

A nationalist movement had developed in Indochina during the Japanese occupation of World War II. So, when the French tried to occupy their colony again, it rebelled. The war in Indochina lasted until 1954 when the French were defeated.

1 The American involvement in Vietnam.

In 1954, after the Geneva treaty, the Americans sent "military advisers" to Vietnam. In 1961, Kennedy substantially increased their number which reached 85 000 in 1964.

On August 7, 1964, Congress announced that the U.S. would support any member state of the SEATO (South East Asia Treaty Organization) asking for aid, even if this meant military involvement. This was the beginning of direct American intervention in Vietnam.

In 1968 there were over 500 000 U.S. soldiers supported by the aircraft carriers of the VIIth fleet. From 1965 on, U.S. planes bombed even North Vietnam.

2 The negotiations

They started in Paris on January 16, 1969, and dragged on until 1973. However, on the eve of the presidential elections, Nixon claimed he intended to withdraw American troops from Vietnam. On January 27, 1973, an agreement was signed, providing for gradual and pacific re-union of the two Vietnams.

3 The aftermath of the Vietnam War

When the agreement had been signed in Paris, the American soldiers were flown back to their country, the P.O.W.s were set free by the North Vietnamese. Apparently, the U.S. had weathered the worst crisis since World War II.

But the Vietnam War has deeply scarred the American conscience. The Americans believe in success, and they have not yet understood how the North Vietnamese could defeat them, in spite of their tremendous military power. Moreover, the war has widened the gap between the young and the adults, the former having taken a firm and early stand against the war.

There results a general and widespread mistrust of traditional adult values, which is, to some extent, responsible for the moral insecurity that many Americans are now experiencing.

to last	durer	**3**	
1		**af**termath	répercussions, conséquences
Geneva	Genève	**flown back**	renvoyés (en avion)
military ad**vi**sers	conseillers militaires	P.O.W.s = **Pri**soners Of **War**	prisonniers de guerre
sub**stan**tially	considérablement	set free	libérés
to **reach**	atteindre	to **wea**ther a **cri**sis	surmonter une crise
SEATO	OTASE (Organisation du Traité de l'Asie du Sud-Est)	to **scar**	laisser des marques sur
		in **spite** of	malgré
to **mean**	signifier	tre**men**dous	formidable
over 500 000	plus de 500 000	has **wi**dened the **gap**	a élargi le fossé
aircraft **car**riers	porte-avions	a **stand**	une position
the VIIth (**Seventh**) **Fleet**	la Septième Flotte	**there re**sults	il s'ensuit
From 1965 **on**	A partir de 1965	**wide**spread	répandu
2		**mistrust** of	défiance envers

OTHER WORDS AND PHRASES

---

to **drag on**	traîner en longueur
on the **eve** of	à la veille de
to in**tend**	avoir l'intention
an a**gree**ment	un accord
provi**ding** for	stipulant qu'il y aurait
gradual	progressive

guer**ri**lla **war**fare	la guérilla, la guerre de partisans
an **am**bush	une embuscade
the ci**vi**lians	les populations civiles
the **un**derground **for**ces	le maquis
a **pup**pet **gov**ernment	un gouvernement fantoche
dic**ta**torship	la dictature
a totali**ta**rian **state**	un État totalitaire

Grammar and exercises

Place des adverbes

1/ **Adverbes de modalité** → le plus souvent devant le mot qu'ils modifient.
   Ex. : — He speaks so fast that I **hardly** understand him.
   — I'm **only half** surprised to see you here.
   — My work is { **almost** } finished.
             { **nearly** }
   — You're **rather** late, aren't you ?

2/ **Adverbes de temps imprécis**   → avant le verbe à un temps simple,
   Adverbes de fréquence   entre l'auxiliaire et le verbe à un temps composé.
   Ex. : — He's **never** been to the United States.
   — They have **already** left.
   — We would **hardly ever** see them if they lived that far.

Cependant ces adverbes se placent après **to be** à un temps simple, sauf si **to be** est le dernier mot de la phrase ou s'il est à l'impératif.
   Ex. : — They're **often** late.
   — "Do you think they'll be late ?"
     "Yes. They **often** are."
   — Let us **never** be late !

D'autre part, on place quelquefois **never** et **always** avant les auxiliaires pour insister.
   Ex. : — I **never** would have accepted under these conditions.

3/ **Adverbes de temps précis** } → généralement en fin de proposition.
   Adverbes de lieu
   Ex. : — We shall certainly go and see them **tomorrow.**

4/ **Autres adverbes (manière, en particulier)** → à divers endroits de la phrase.

5/ **Enough, too much :** { après le verbe } qu'ils modifient.
                          { avant le nom }
   Enough : après l'adjectif qu'il modifie.

6/ **Very much, (very) well, badly :** en fin de proposition, sauf si le complément est très long.

7/ **also :** avant le verbe (temps simple).
   entre auxiliaire et verbe (temps composé).

THE UNITED STATES IN THE WORLD

Put the adverb in the correct place in order to modify the underlined word:

1 ALMOST: The military aid the U.S. gave the Allied forces was <u>unlimited</u>.
2 JUST: At the end of 1941, the U.S. <u>had entered</u> the war.
3 QUITE: When Germany capitulated, the atomic bomb was not <u>ready</u>.
4 EVEN: <u>The Americans</u> were surprised by the destructive power of the atomic bomb.
5 COMPLETELY: The American fleet was <u>destroyed</u> in Pearl Harbour.
6 SLOWLY BUT STEADILY: From 1943 on, the Americans <u>progressed</u>.
7 USUALLY: After an air raid over an island, the marines <u>stormed</u> the position.
8 ALREADY: In 1945, most of the Philippines <u>was reconquered</u>.
9 ON JUNE 6,1944: The Allied forces landed on the shores of Normandy.
10 NEVER: Some people argue that the U.S. <u>should have used</u> the atomic bomb.
11 HARDLY EVER: I <u>am</u> tired.
12 ENOUGH: There were not <u>dug-outs</u> to protect the civilians.
13 ENOUGH: I think you have not <u>worked</u> to pass your exam.
14 ENOUGH: He is not <u>old</u> to see that film.
15 ALSO: NATO <u>was created</u> after World War II.
16 VERY MUCH: We <u>appreciated</u> that film about World War II and its aftermath.
17 VERY MUCH: We <u>enjoyed</u> that film.
18 NEARLY: The Cuban missile crisis <u>led</u> to a war.
19 OFFICIALLY: The Korean war <u>was conducted</u> by the UN.
20 UNFORTUNATELY: He <u>was killed</u> before he could carry out the reforms he had promised.
21 AT TEN O'CLOCK, TOMORROW: He'll receive you.
22 NO LONGER: The Presidency <u>enjoys</u> the same prestige.
23 SUBSTANTIALLY: In 1961, Kennedy <u>increased</u> the number of American military advisers in Vietnam.
24 DEEPLY: The Vietnam War <u>has scarred</u> the American conscience.
25 NOW: Many Americans <u>are experiencing</u> some moral insecurity.

Place de l'adjectif

1/ **L'adjectif épithète** se place avant le nom.

Cependant :
a/ épithète accompagné d'un complément :

— A **full** bus arrived.

mais : — A bus **full** of people arrived.

b/ Plusieurs épithètes :

— A **clean-shaven** young man.

mais : — A **respectable-looking young** man, **clean-shaven** and **well-dressed,** came to the office this morning.

c/ Expressions toutes faites :

Ex. : — the heir **apparent** : *l'héritier présomptif.*
— the sum **total** : *le total (d'une addition).*

2/ **L'adjectif attribut** se place après le verbe quand il se rapporte au sujet de ce verbe, ou après le complément auquel il se rapporte.

— He is **exhausted.**
— She looks **pretty.**
— The jurors declared the boy **guilty.**

L'adjectif peut accompagner **something, anything, nothing** sans préposition :

— I've been told something **funny.**
(On m'a raconté quelque chose d'amusant.)

Note : Rappelons que L'ADJECTIF EST INVARIABLE.

THE UNITED STATES IN THE WORLD

A *Make sentences with the following words and phrases:*

1 kept receiving / aid / military / the Allied / from the U.S. / forces.
2 numerous / substantial / sent to Great Britain / the / were a / help / weapons.
3 aim of Japan / to dominate / was / Asia / Eastern / the / obvious.
4 did not play / in the war / a / the United States / part / passive / merely.
5 who think / should / in Vietnam / there are / far / Americans / too many / that the atomic bomb / been used / have.

B *Put the adjective in the correct place:*

1 HORRIFIC: The atomic bomb is a <u>weapon</u>.
2 VERY POLITE: He is a <u>salesman</u> with customers.
3 ROYAL: The <u>Princess</u> was present at their party.
4 WELL-SPOKEN, PRETTY, WELL-DRESSED: A young <u>woman</u> told me this.
5 ASLEEP: Look at our <u>children</u> in their little beds.
6 SLEEPING: We must not wake up those <u>children</u>.
7 AVAILABLE: Give me a list of the <u>goods</u>.
8 PRETTIER: Have you ever read a <u>story</u>?
9 KIND: I know he is a <u>man</u> to his fellow-men.
10 MERE: The <u>thought</u> of what he did fills me with horror.
11 ALIVE: They are the nicest <u>people</u>.
12 INTELLIGENT: Though <u>he</u> may be, it was stupid of him to say this.
13 WISE: Experience makes <u>men</u>.
14 ENVIOUS: She is a <u>woman</u> of other people.
15 WIDE: The <u>lane</u> is only three feet.
16 JEALOUS: My brother is a <u>man</u> of the people who work with him.
17 NEW: Did they announce <u>anything</u> on the radio?
18 ALONE: I don't mind living and dying.

L'article défini

The est un ancien démonstratif. Il a donc une valeur beaucoup plus forte que l'article défini en français.

Emploi : a/ les noms dénombrables se construisent au singulier avec un article défini ou indéfini.

b/ pour les dénombrables au pluriel et les indénombrables (qui sont toujours au singulier), on emploie l'article quand le nom est déterminé par une proposition, un complément de nom, un adjectif ou le contexte, ou par leur sens même (mots désignant une chose unique en son genre, une institution, une catégorie, etc...).

A *Use the definite article if necessary:*

1 In ... United States ... conflict between ... Blacks and ... Whites is by no means over.
2 In ... South, ... white people have always protested against ... desegregation.
3 ... slavery was abolished over a century ago.
4 Some Black militants proclaim that "... Black is beautiful."
5 ... blue of your dress is lovely.
6 ... English is not a difficult language.
7 ... English they speak in America is different from ... English spoken by ... British.
8 ... influence of ... Protestantism over ... Americans has been deep and enduring.
9 ... importance attached to ... education and ... leisure testifies to ... development of a society.
10 There are now many Americans suffering from ... poverty and ... unemployment.
11 ... unemployment now prevailing in industrialized countries is alarming.
12 I listen to ... radio, I go to ... cinema, I use ... telephone and I read ... press. But I do not watch ... television.
13 ... Queen Elizabeth I played a major role in ... British history (= in ... history of Britain).
14 ... President delivered a very uninteresting Inaugural Address.
15 This young boy wants to enter ... Police, ... Army or ... Navy when he is older.

B *Use the definite or indefinite article when necessary:*

1 I read ... detective novel and ... science fiction one, and I liked ... both.
2 ... novel is ... most popular literary genre.
3 ... business is ... business.
4 ... dog is ... friend of ... man.
5 Some men say it is impossible to understand ... women.
6 I love to spend my holidays in ... England.
7 ... England I love is ... England of ... 18th century, ... rural England.
8 Baldwin, ... Black writer of talent, helps us to understand ... reactions of ... American Blacks.
9 ... rebellion and ... violence are manifestations of ... moral crisis in ... America.
10 We play ... tennis on ... Sundays.
11 He always speaks ... truth.
12 ... last year, I went to ... America, and ... next year, I'll go to ... Africa. I'm interested in ... both continents.
13 What ... pity you cannot come to ... States with me!
14 What ... contempt ... Whites show for ... Blacks!
15 When I was ... child, ... President, ... very simple man, came to our city.
16 ... mass media have such ... influence on ... silent majority!
17 Unemployment is as important ... problem for us as it is for you.
18 I'll be ready in half ... hour.
19 This businessman goes to New York twice ... month.
20 ... Americans have ... guilty conscience where ... Blacks and ... Indians are concerned.
21 He's got ... headache and ... sore throat: he must have ... flu.
22 Considering what ... wages are in this country, ... workers have ... right to complain.
23 ... English are said to have ... sense of ... humour.
24 I'm at ... loss as to how to put ... end to this affair.
25 ... teenagers must study ... modern languages.

Le passif

1 / Formation : **to be** (conjugué) + **participe passé**

2 / Verbes à double passif (verbes suivis d'un complément d'attribution et d'un complément d'objet) :

— They gave him a chair.
→ a / **A chair was given to him.**
  b / **He was given a chair.**

3 / Verbes suivis d'une postposition ou d'un complément indirect introduit par une préposition :

— They'll put off the meeting.
→ **The meeting will be put off.**
— They'll send for the doctor.
→ **The doctor will be sent for.**

Rappelons que le passif est très fréquemment l'équivalent anglais du « on » français.
— *On m'a dit que vous alliez à Londres.*

I've been told that you were going to London.

Like and as

Like (préposition) → suivi d'un nom ou d'un pronom, éventuellement accompagnés d'adverbes ou d'adjectifs.
As (conjonction et pronom relatif) → introduit une proposition complète ou elliptique.
— *Je pense comme vous.*

2 traductions :
  a / I think **like** you.
  b / I think **as** you do.

Note : Dans la proposition introduite par **as,** le verbe peut être omis :

— Her children lead an independent life, **as** in America.
= **as** children do in America.

THE UNITED STATES IN THE WORLD

A *Turn the following sentences into the passive voice:*

1 He beats her every day.
2 She began the story an hour ago.
3 They are binding their prisoner to a tree.
4 They have broken the table.
5 They are building a house.
6 They had given him an award.
7 They sent their parents a letter.
8 She teaches the pupils English.
9 She tells her children a story.
10 I can't put up with this attitude.
11 They took the chairs away.
12 She often keeps the children in.
13 They were putting down what the lecturer said.
14 The drunkard flung the bottle violently.
15 We've thought over the problem.
16 They've read your letter through carefully.
17 He put forward amazing arguments to convince us.
18 People eat a lot of fruit in summer.
19 Everybody finds her very pretty.
20 She was speaking to them in a very rude manner.

B *Use LIKE or AS in the following sentences:*

1 ... their parents, American children join clubs.
2 I'm a member of this club, ... are my parents.
3 Do ... you like.
4 Everything happened ... I told you.
5 You certainly don't live ... we do.
6 You certainly don't live ... us.
7 The children were running ... the devil from the house on fire.
8 He was pacing up and down ... a caged beast.
9 It's because the poor would like to live ... the rich that they feel dissatisfied.
10 Don't do ... I do; do ... I tell you to do.

Test

1
- ☐ a/ Never I have read such a stupid book
- ☐ b/ I have read such a stupid book never
- ☐ c/ I have read never such a stupid book
- ☐ d/ I have never read such a stupid book

2
- ☐ a/ Substantially their income has increased
- ☐ b/ Their income has increased substantially
- ☐ c/ Their income substantially has increased
- ☐ d/ Their substantially income has increased

3 Peter and Mary ....
- ☐ a/ often play with John
- ☐ b/ play often with John
- ☐ c/ play with John often
- ☐ d/ would play often with John

4
- ☐ a/ We shall see you at your office tomorrow
- ☐ b/ We shall tomorrow at your office see you
- ☐ c/ We shall tomorrow see you at your office
- ☐ d/ We shall at your office see you tomorrow

5 Last summer, we went to India, ...
- ☐ a/ and also we went to Japan
- ☐ b/ and we also went to Japan
- ☐ c/ and we too went to Japan
- ☐ d/ and we went to also Japan

6
- ☐ a/ There's an astray dog on the road
- ☐ b/ There's a dog on the road astray
- ☐ c/ There's a dog on the astray road
- ☐ d/ There's a dog astray on the road

7 She was wearing ....
- ☐ a/ a blue hat feather-covered
- ☐ b/ a blue covered with feathers hat
- ☐ c/ a hat blue covered with feathers
- ☐ d/ a blue hat covered with feathers

8
- ☐ a/ The jurors declared the guilty defendant
- ☐ b/ The jurors declared the defendant guilty
- ☐ c/ The guilty jurors declared the defendant
- ☐ d/ The jurors guilty declared the defendant

THE UNITED STATES IN THE WORLD 139

9 Many people are against ... atomic bomb.
  ☐ a/ a use of
  ☐ b/ use of
  ☐ c/ the use of the
  ☐ d/ the use of

10 ... remorse makes him very unhappy
  ☐ a/ Some
  ☐ b/ The
  ☐ c/ An
  ☐ d/ —

11 ... remorse he felt after killing his wife did not seem very deep.
  ☐ a/ Some
  ☐ b/ The
  ☐ c/ An
  ☐ d/ —

12 ... President Kennedy was long considered as an exceptional man.
  ☐ a/ The
  ☐ b/ —
  ☐ c/ Some
  ☐ d/ An

13 We were proud that ... President should have visited our town.
  ☐ a/ some
  ☐ b/ an
  ☐ c/ the
  ☐ d/ —

14 She is ... her sister.
  ☐ a/ as beautiful girl as
  ☐ b/ as beautiful the girl as
  ☐ c/ as beautiful a girl as
  ☐ d/ beautiful girl as

15 Pupils study ... modern languages at ... school.
  ☐ a/ — / —
  ☐ b/ — / the
  ☐ c/ the / —
  ☐ d/ the / the

16 ... United Kingdom includes ... England, ... Wales, ... Scotland and ... Northern Ireland.
  ☐ a/ The / — / the / — / the
  ☐ b/ — / — / — / — / —
  ☐ c/ The / the / the / the / the
  ☐ d/ The / — / — / — / —

17 What ... influence such ... magazine has on the silent majority!
  ☐ a/ an / —
  ☐ b/ — / a
  ☐ c/ — / —
  ☐ d/ a / a

18 They have a big house ... their parents'.
  ☐ a/ as
  ☐ b/ as if
  ☐ c/ like
  ☐ d/ as like

140 GRAMMAR AND EXERCISES

19 I simply couldn't work day in day out ... you do.
  □ a/ as
  □ b/ as though
  □ c/ as much
  □ d/ like

20 I'll never be rich ... him.
  □ a/ as
  □ b/ like
  □ c/ as like
  □ d/ —

THE UNITED STATES IN THE WORLD

A *Translate into English:*

1 Les Américains n'essayèrent la bombe atomique qu'une fois avant de l'utiliser au Japon.
2 On n'avait jamais utilisé la bombe auparavant.
3 Presque aussitôt après les Japonais capitulèrent.
4 Les Japonais ne furent pas les seuls à être horrifiés.
5 Avez-vous jamais entendu parler des armes biologiques?
6 Ils n'en avaient jamais entendu parler.
7 Les pertes en hommes sont toujours importantes dans une guerre comme la seconde guerre mondiale.
8 On n'a jamais enrayé une attaque de cette manière.
9 La ville fut entièrement détruite par les bombardements.
10 Ils avaient déjà bombardé la moitié du pays.

B *Translate into English:*

1 Ils sont toujours prêts à se battre contre quiconque les attaquera.
2 Je suis toujours surprise quand j'entends de telles affirmations.
3 N'avez-vous jamais peur quand vous voyez quelles armes terribles on produit?
4 Ne soyons jamais trop pessimistes!
5 J'ai toujours soif pendant les repas.

C *Translate into English:*

1 Nous partons pour les États-Unis après-demain.
2 Ils se sont rencontrés par hasard avant-hier chez des amis.
3 J'avais été entièrement convaincu par leurs arguments.
4 Nous avons beaucoup aimé ce film.
5 Ils n'ont pas beaucoup aimé ce livre qui raconte la vie d'une famille américaine pendant la guerre.

D *Translate into English:*

1 Nous n'avons jamais assez d'argent pour joindre les deux bouts.
2 Ils n'avaient pas assez de soldats pour se défendre.
3 Vous n'êtes pas assez optimiste.
4 Mais lui est trop pessimiste.
5 J'ai trop de travail.
6 Trop de soldats ont été tués.
7 Ils ne sont pas assez décidés.
8 Ils ne se sont pas décidés assez vite.

E *Translate into English:*

1 Ce ne fut pas un président remarquable.
2 Cette guerre fut particulièrement cruelle.
3 La C.I.A. est demeurée puissante et ses interventions excessives.
4 Je n'ai rien vu de remarquable dans cet homme.
5 On dit pourtant qu'il a fait quelque chose d'étonnant.
6 Avez-vous jamais vu un film plus intéressant?
7 Il y a quelque chose qui ne va pas.
8 On l'a déclaré coupable.

F *Translate into English:*

1 Il y a des gens endormis dans cette pièce.
2 J'aime me promener seul.
3 Regardez ce bateau à la dérive sur le fleuve.
4 Il était étendu, éveillé, sur son lit.
5 C'est une femme jalouse de la beauté des autres femmes.
6 C'est une épouse jalouse.
7 La pièce a 30 pieds de long sur 20 pieds de large.
8 Cette histoire est vieille de plusieurs siècles.

G *Translate into English:*

1 Ils ont été tués par les ennemis.
2 On dit qu'ils ont été tués par les ennemis.
3 On m'a dit que vous aviez l'intention de donner votre démission.
4 On lui avait dit que sa popularité serait accrue.
5 On m'a raconté quelque chose de très drôle.
6 Le mythe présidentiel a été terni par ce scandale.
7 Cuba n'a pas été reconquise par les exilés qui ont débarqué en 1961.
8 On était en train d'élaborer une nouvelle arme.
9 On était en train d'envahir l'île.
10 On était en train de reconquérir les Philippines.

H *Translate into English:*

1 Nous vivons comme des Américains. Nous vivons comme en Amérique.
2 Je suis jeune et travailleur comme lui.
3 Elle était charmante et bien élevée comme sa sœur.
4 Je vais réagir comme vous l'avez fait à leur proposition.
5 Je ferai comme vous voudrez.

1 The consumer society

The necessity to create demand in order to find outlets for mass-produced goods has led to the creation of artificial needs among the population through advertising.

1 Advertising
The purpose of advertising is to sell to the greatest number of customers. To this end, it must be persuasive, but it must also attract and retain the attention of the customer.
Posters, road signs and the display of goods in shopwindows are traditional means of attracting attention.
But, nowadays, a wider use is made of the mass media (i.e. the press, television, and the radio) to convince the public. Thus, most TV and radio programmes are interrupted by commercials, and newspapers are covered with ads extolling the merits of goods and services.
By appealing to our senses, feelings, frustrations and yearnings, by taking advantage of our shortcomings, advertising turns us into compulsive buyers for the benefit of the industrial society. The affluent society becomes a consumer society. This is the reason why advertising has become such a controversial issue.

2 Waste making
But advertising is not sufficient to avoid the prospect of glutted markets. So other devices must be contrived to force people to buy more and more.
Thus the quality of the goods has kept deteriorating over the years. The emphasis has been laid on fashion which causes models of the previous years to look outmoded. People have been convinced that they must "keep up with the Joneses". And, finally, the development of credit facilities, with the possibility of buying on instalment plans, has greatly contributed to increasing consumption.

3 Consumer protection
Ralph Nader initiated the movement when he denounced the automanufacturers in the U.S. and demanded greater safety. Since then, the movement has kept gathering momentum and individual consumers now form local and national organizations. In addition, a growing number of journalists have become the spokesmen of the consumers. But much still remains to be done if the latter are to be protected against misleading advertising and dishonest practices.

A FEW PROBLEMS OF THE CONTEMPORARY WORLD 145

a con**su**mer	un consommateur
the con**su**mer so**ci**ety	la société de consommation
de**mand**	la demande
an **out**let	un débouché
through	au moyen de
ad**vert**ising	la publicité

1

a **cus**tomer	un client
to this **end**	dans ce dessein
per**sua**sive	persuasif
a **pos**ter	une affiche
a **road sign**	un panneau routier
dis**play**	exposition, étalage
a **shop**window	une vitrine
a **means**	un moyen
the **mass me**dia	les moyens de communication de masse
a com**mer**cial	une annonce publicitaire
ads = ad**ver**tisements (1)	réclames
to ex**tol**	vanter, louer
a **yearn**ing	une aspiration
to **take** ad**van**tage of	tirer profit de
a short**com**ing	un défaut
a com**pul**sive **buy**er	quelqu'un qui ne peut s'empêcher d'acheter
the **af**fluent so**ci**ety	la société de l'abondance
a contro**ver**sial **is**sue	un sujet disputé

2

waste making	le gaspillage
to a**void**	éviter
glutted	encombré
a de**vice**	un expédient
con**trived**	imaginé, inventé
has kept de**te**riorating	n'a cessé de décroître
previous	précédent
out**mo**ded	démodé
to **keep up** with the **Jo**neses	faire concurrence aux voisins
on ins**tal**ment **plans**	à crédit

3

to **ga**ther mo**men**tum	acquérir de la force
in ad**di**tion	de plus
a **spokes**man	un porte-parole
the **lat**ter	ces derniers
mis**lead**ing	trompeuse, fallacieuse

OTHER WORDS AND PHRASES

offer	l'offre
con**sump**tion	la consommation
a **month**ly ins**tal**ment	une mensualité (pour achat à crédit)
planned obso**les**cence	la planification du vieillissement des produits

---

1. Prononciation britannique. Aux États-Unis : ad**ver**tisements → ads.

2 Environment and pollution

One of the major plagues of our industrial societies is the fouling of air, land and water both in cities and in the country.

1 Pollution in cities
In most cities, noxious fumes emanating from the exhaust pipes of cars and from factory smokestacks are suspended in the air above industrial cities.
Pollution blankets cause the death of many people in winter. The sewers release into the rivers wastes made up of organic material as well as non-biodegradable synthetic detergents which cause irreparable harm.

2 Pollution in the country
Because manpower is often cheaper in the country, many small manufacturers set up factories on the outskirts of small towns.
The rivers are often spoilt by foam resulting from industrial wastes. Foul-smelling vapours poison the air and sewage contaminates water.

3 Atomic pollution
On a worldwide scale, atomic tests pollute the air. Radioactive particles are released into the atmosphere. Nuclear fallout is responsible for some birth defects.
A nuclear test ban was signed in 1963 but tests are still conducted in several countries.

4 The consequences and the remedies
Air pollution is responsible for lung disease (the lung cancer rate is twice as high in the cities as in the country).
Water pollution threatens the life of fish; swimming has become dangerous in most rivers and even the beaches (particularly those of closed seas, such as the Mediterranean) are spoilt. Thanks to the dire warnings of the ecologists, more and more people have woken up to the necessity to take drastic steps in order to fight environmental pollution.
Anti-pollution devices, filters, recycling of wastes and rubbish have been adopted by industrialists willing to cope with the problem. But only governmental measures can be truly effective.

A FEW PROBLEMS OF THE CONTEMPORARY WORLD 147

a **pla**gue	un fléau
fouling	encrassement, pollution

1

no**x**ious **fumes**	vapeurs toxiques
an ex**haust pipe**	un tuyau d'échappement
fac**tory smoke**stacks	cheminées d'usines
a **blan**ket	une couverture
the **sew**ers	les égouts
to re**lease**	décharger
harm	dommage

2

manpower	la main-d'œuvre
cheaper	meilleur marché
a manu**fac**turer	un petit industriel
outskirts	faubourgs
foam	écume
wastes	déchets
foul-**smell**ing	nauséabond
sewage	les eaux d'égouts

3

on a **world**wide **scale**	à l'échelle mondiale
nuclear **fall**out	les retombées radioactives
birth de**fects**	défauts de naissance
a **ban**	une interdiction

4

a **re**medy	un remède
the **lung**	le poumon
twice as **high** ... as	deux fois plus élevé... que
to **threat**en	menacer
the **beach**es	les plages
dire	très graves, désespérés
a **warn**ing	un avertissement
to **wake up** to	prendre conscience de
drastic **steps**	des mesures drastiques
a **fil**ter	un filtre
re**cy**cling of **wastes**	recyclage des déchets
rubbish	détritus
an in**dus**trialist	un industriel
willing to	prêts à
to **cope** with	faire face à
truly	réellement
ef**fec**tive	efficace

OTHER WORDS AND PHRASES

chemicals	produits chimiques
toxic **fumes**	vapeurs toxiques
filth	la crasse
garbage **dumps**	dépôts d'ordures
to **dump**	déverser
conser**va**tion	la protection de la nature
a conser**va**tionist	un défenseur de la nature

3 Population growth

The accelerated growth rate of the world population after World War II has caused increasing concern among governments and authorities of all nations.

1 Population planning in developed industrialized nations
In spite of the gravity of the issue, it is never really acute in industrialized nations. These countries have developed birth-control techniques (the pill, for instance) as well as liberalized their legislation (abortion has become legal in many developed countries).

Family planning is made comparatively easy through mass-produced and readily accessible contraceptive methods and information. Thus population growth is, to some extent, regularized.

2 The developing nations
It is in the nations which have not as yet reached a high standard of living that the population explosion raises the most critical problems for the spectre of hunger haunts these nations.

Various plans to slow down the rate of population growth have been worked out: education, information, and facilitated family planning.

Birth-control policies have been implemented by various governments. In India, for instance, the government gives inducements in the form of free gifts and bonuses to all fathers of three who undergo a sterilizing operation.

3 Moral problems raised by population control
According to some, overpopulation is a myth invented by the rich (determined to preserve their standard of living) to subjugate and exploit the poor.

To people holding this opinion, birth-control will be of no avail if rich industrialized nations waste the natural resources of the world by overconsumption.

They denounce the attitude of the rich nations which deny the poorer nations the right to procreate.

Policies and plans are needed which cut across national borders to deal with the problems on a worldwide scale. Aid has to be provided to developing nations to achieve a minimum basic standard of living for everyone.

growth	croissance
growth rate	taux de croissance
con**cern**	inquiétude

1

the **is**sue	le problème
a**cute**	aigu
birth-control	contrôle des naissances
the **pill**	la pilule
as **well** as	ainsi que
a**bor**tion	l'avortement
com**pa**ratively	relativement
readily ac**ces**sible	facilement accessible
to **some** ex**tent**	dans une certaine mesure

2

a de**ve**loping **na**tion	un pays en voie de développement
not (as) **yet**	pas encore
to **reach**	atteindre
to **raise**	soulever
for	car
hunger	la faim
to **haunt**	hanter
to **slow down**	freiner
worked out	exécuté, mené à bien
a **po**licy	une politique (1)
implemented	mis en œuvre
an in**duce**ment	un encouragement
a **bo**nus	une prime
to **un**de**rgo**	subir

3

ac**cord**ing to **some**	selon certains
to **sub**jugate	assujettir
holding this o**pi**nion	qui ont cette opinion
of no a**vail**	sans effet
to **waste**	gaspiller
o**ver**con**sump**tion	la surconsommation
de**ny** the **poo**rer **na**tions the **right** to	refusent aux pays plus pauvres le droit de
to **cut** a**cross na**tional **bor**ders	ne pas tenir compte des frontières
to a**chieve**	réussir, réaliser

---

1. **politics**: la politique.

4   Hunger in the world

In the 18th century, Malthus predicted that world population would some day outrun man's capacity to produce food.
A few days before his death, Adlai Stevenson addressed the United Nations' Economic and Social Council with the warning: "We travel together, passengers on a little spaceship, dependent on its vulnerable supplies of air and soil…"
It is needless to emphasize that this notion of « spaceship Earth" also applies to food and energy.

1 The starving or threatened areas
Nearly half a billion people are suffering from some form of hunger. There are the all too familiar shortages of food in the Sahel. Only slightly less serious are the situations in Honduras, Burma, Burundi, Rwanda, the Sudan and Yemen.
Poor harvests threaten food supplies in Nepal, Somalia, Tanzania, and Zambia.
In Haiti, because of disregard for soil conservation, hundreds of thousands of subsistence farmers face starvation.

2 The disasters of the past years
Bad crops forced the surplus-producing nations to curtail the amounts of relief food the normally send as aid to the hungry nations. To this must be added the dwindling fish supplies resulting from sea pollution.
Short supplies of cereals and protein-yielding fish coincided with drought conditions in the threatened areas, causing famine. As a consequence, many people starved to death. Pictures of emaciated adults and children, their bones piercing through their skin, gave a guilty conscience to the populations of the affluent societies.

3 Attempts at remedying the situation
When famine was ravaging hundreds of millions of the poorest people in at least 40 nations, the delegates from 100 nations and several international organizations gathered in Rome for the World Food Conference in a concerted global effort to confront the problem of hunger. But all the aid the starving nations got from the Conference was rhetoric… not much for empty stomachs! Moreover, though relief food was sent from all over the world, the authorities often proved incompetent, failing to assure efficient and rapid distribution. Millions of people starved to death while we were overconsuming in our affluent societies.

A FEW PROBLEMS OF THE CONTEMPORARY WORLD

to out**r**un	aller plus vite que
a **warn**ing	un avertissement
a **space**ship	un vaisseau spatial
it is **need**less to **em**phasize	il est inutile de souligner
to ap**ply** to	s'appliquer à

1

to **starve**	1 / souffrir de la faim 2 / affamer
threatened	menacé
a **bil**lion	un milliard de
all too	que trop
shortage	pénurie
Burma	la Birmanie
poor harvests	récoltes médiocres
dis**re**gard	négligence
sub**sis**tence **farm**ers	paysans que leur récolte nourrit à peine

2

to cur**tail**	réduire
re**lief food**	produits alimentaires de secours
dwindling	en diminution
re**sul**ting from	dû à
protein-yielding	riches en protéines
drought	la sécheresse
to **starve** to **death**	mourir de faim
e**ma**ciated	décharné
bones	os
a **guil**ty **con**science	un sentiment de culpabilité

3

an at**tempt**	une tentative
to **re**medy	porter remède à
at **least**	au moins
to **ga**ther	se réunir
empty **sto**machs	des ventres vides
to **prove** in**com**petent	se révéler incompétent
failing to as**sure**	n'assurant pas
ef**fi**cient	efficace
to **o**vercon**sume**	surconsommer

OTHER WORDS AND PHRASES

---

a **boun**teous (= **bum**per) **crop**	une récolte très importante
soya**bean**	le soja
foodstuffs	les produits alimentaires
scarcity	pénurie
under**fed**	sous-alimenté
famished	affamé
famine-**strick**en	touché par la famine
malnutrition	la sous-alimentation
scurvy	le scorbut

5 The energy crisis

With the sudden decision of the OPEC nations to raise oil prices, many industrialized countries have become aware of the need to save energy sources.

1 Petroleum or oil
Oil-wells are drilled wherever oil has been found. Oil is then pumped out of the subsoil. Then it is conveyed to distant places in pipelines. If it is to be transported overseas, this is done by oil-tankers (many giant tankers are built in Japan).
On reaching its place of destination, crude oil is processed in a refinery. Thus gasoline for car engines is produced.
It is carried to the gas-stations in tank trucks.
In addition to being a raw material for motor fuel, oil is used for the production of petrochemicals: plastics, synthetic fibres, artificial fertilizers, insecticides, cosmetics.
Fuel oil distillate is used for heating homes.

2 Other sources of energy
The Middle East oil-producing nations account for more than 60 % of total world reserves. When, at the instigation of these nations, the OPEC countries raised their oil prices, the importing nations intensified the search for alternative sources of energy.
Closed coal-mines have been reopened, oil shales are being prospected.
Architects are developing projects for homes that will be heated by solar energy.
But there is little doubt that, so long as no other source of energy is found, the governments of most nations will favour the development of nuclear energy. At present there does not seem to be any alternative.
However, the risks incurred disturb people all over the world.

3 The political consequences of the crisis
Although they do not always agree on the attitude to adopt, the affluent importing nations (the U.S., Western Europe and Japan) have attempted to set up a common policy to meet the challenge. For them the crisis has not brought about disaster. But for the poorest non-oil-producing nations (the Fourth World), the situation is far more serious for they cannot afford to buy oil in quantities sufficient to develop their economy. Thus their growth is threatened and, at best, will be delayed.

A FEW PROBLEMS OF THE CONTEMPORARY WORLD 153

OPEC (Organization of Petroleum Exporting Countries)	OPEP (Organisation des Pays Exportateurs de Pétrole)
to **raise**	relever (1)
aware of	conscient de

1

pe**tro**leum (GB) = **oil** (US)	le pétrole
an **oil-well**	un puits de pétrole
to **drill**	forer
the **sub**soil	le sous-sol
to con**vey**	transporter
over**seas**	au-delà des mers
crude (oil)	(pétrole) brut
processed	traité
gasoline = **gas** (US) = **pe**trol (GB)	l'essence
a **gas**-station (US) = **fill**ing-station (GB)	une station service
a **tank truck**	un camion citerne
a mo**to**r **fuel**	un carburant
petro**che**micals	produits pétrochimiques
fertilizers	engrais
cos**me**tics	produits de parfumerie
distillate	produit de distillation

2

the **Middle East**	le Moyen-Orient
ac**count** for	représentent
at the insti**ga**tion of	à l'instigation de
al**ter**native (adj.)	autre(s)
oil shales	schistes bitumineux
so **long** as	tant que
an al**ter**native (noun)	1 / une autre solution 2 / une alternative
in**cur**red	encourus

3

a **chall**enge	un défi
the **Fourth World**	le Quart Monde
serious	grave
they **cannot** af**ford**	ils ne peuvent se permettre
growth	la croissance
at **best**	dans la meilleure hypothèse
de**layed**	retardé(e)

---

1. Ne pas confondre avec to **rise, rose, risen** : s'élever.
Ex. : **Oil prices have been raised** : On a relevé les prix du pétrole.
  Oil prices have risen : Les prix du pétrole ont monté.

Grammar and exercises

Structures verbales

A *Use the infinitive (with or without "to"):*

1 TO TALK: He asked ... to the boss.
2 TO BE: She deserves ... rewarded.
3 TO ATTEND: He has refused ... the meeting.
4 TO CALL: You may ... on them now if you like.
5 TO DO: They failed ... their duty.
6 TO SOLVE: He endeavoured ... their problems.
7 TO LEAVE: We'd better ... now.
8 TO STAY: We'd rather ... .
9 TO WORK: You needn't ... so hard.
10 TO DO: What do you intend ... ?
11 TO SEE: He said he wished ... them now.
12 TO TAKE: They've decided ... measures against polluters.
13 TO HELP: I mean ... them.
14 TO HAVE: You should ... taken this into account.
15 TO SAY: You mustn't ... such nasty things to her.

B *Use the infinitive (with or without "to"):*

1 TO SAY: She always makes me ... what I don't want ... .
2 TO DO: He is a spoilt child: his parents let him ... what he likes.
3 TO BE: A man had called on you, and he turned out ... your brother-in-law.
4 TO COME: They didn't tell me not ... .
5 TO BE: She is said ... fond of children.
6 TO ARRIVE: We're waiting for them ... .
7 TO BUY: They are poor and can't afford ... such expensive things.
8 TO WRITE: I ought ... the report now.
9 TO DRINK: She does not want her husband ... so much.

A FEW PROBLEMS OF THE CONTEMPORARY WORLD 155

10 TO SWIM: She teaches her children ... .
11 TO TAKE: Why don't you get him ... a decision.
12 TO SPEAK: She had him ... the truth.
13 TO KNOW/TO COME: Let us ... when you want us ... .
14 TO JUMP: I saw the child ... from the tree.
15 TO JUMP: The child was seen ... from the tree.
16 TO SHOUT: The neighbours heard her ... for help.
17 TO SHOUT: She was heard ... for help.
18 TO SING: They made the little girl ... a nursery rhyme.
19 TO SING: She was made ... a nursery rhyme.
20 TO HAND IN: We've compelled him ... his resignation.

C *Use the infinitive, gerund or present participle:*

1 TO LOOK AFTER: They offered ... our children.
2 TO MAKE: He always avoids ... efforts.
3 TO SAY: Can you forgive her ... that?
4 TO DO: I remember ... that when I was a child.
5 TO DO: You must remember ... your work tomorrow.
6 TO STAY: He ordered them ... .
7 TO TAKE: We can't put off ... drastic measures.
8 TO SEND: They expect the rich nations ... them relief food.
9 TO HELP: Would you mind ... me?
10 TO BE: I can't stand ... talked to like that.
11 TO FLY: They contemplate ... to the States.
12 TO HAVE: I enjoy ... all my children around.
13 TO RAISE: He has agreed ... his workers' wages.
14 TO WALK: Can you see John ... down the street?
15 TO DISAPPEAR: I saw the thief ... round the corner.
16 TO BE: He is believed ... a first-rate journalist.
17 TO SUCCEED: We trust him ... in this difficult task.
18 TO SING: I heard them ... all afternoon.
19 TO DO: I'm sure they expected us ... the job.
20 TO FLY/TO SAIL: I prefer ... to ... .

D *Use the correct preposition when a preposition is necessary:*

1 She always laughs ... people.
2 She laughed ... a very nasty laugh.
3 His boss praised him ... his achievements.
4 They always reproach ... their child ... something.
5 Fear prevented them ... going.
6 Give ... me this book, don't give it ... Peter.
7 I said: give ... it ... me.
8 "Will you lend ... me this book?"
"No, I'll lend it ... Peter."
9 How could he play such a nasty trick ... us?
10 He's trusted ... me ... all his money.
11 The OPEC nations supply ... us ... oil.
12 The doctor has been sent ... .
13 He is charged ... having stolen the money.
14 He is accused ... having stolen the money.
15 Thank you ... helping me out of my difficulties.
16 On Mothers'Day she was presented ... a lovely scarf.
17 We've been robbed ... all our valuables.
18 We congratulate you ... your choice.
19 How much did you borrow ... the bank?
20 Don't hide the truth ... me.

E *Use the correct preposition when a preposition is necessary:*

1 English is not a language that can be dispensed ... .
2 Why does she pride herself ... being beautiful?
3 We were hoping ... them to come.
4 Isn't there any hope ... their coming?
5 They met ... so many difficulties that they nearly gave up.
6 He succeeds ... all his undertakings.
7 Why do you insist ... such a course of action?
8 What you're telling us doesn't fit in ... what we already know.
9 I'm sure your parents will approve ... your behaviour.
10 Excuse us ... being so late.
11 His secretary had to remind him ... the appointment.

A FEW PROBLEMS OF THE CONTEMPORARY WORLD 157

12 In order to meet ... their needs in energy many countries must import oil from the Middle East.
13 Don't laugh ... people: it is rude; smile ... them, that's what is done.
14 Japan depends ... imports of oil.
15 They inflicted a punishment ... their child.

F *Use the correct preposition when a preposition is necessary:*

1 I'm really interested ... foreign languages.
2 Don't forget to extol ... his merits and to praise him ... them.
3 Don't you think the President's assertions need commenting ... ?
4 She is beaming ... pleasure and laughing ... joy.
5 What policy have you agreed ... ?
6 Not only did you choose the wrong policy but you persist ... your choice!
7 What do you intend to specialize ... ?
8 Will the chairman be here to preside ... the meeting?
9 They've been living ... bread and water for several days.
10 The salesgirl should be attending ... the customers.
11 Who attended ... the meeting?
12 I can't answer ... you.
13 I'm afraid the date you mention doesn't suit ... me.
14 Listen ... what she is saying.
15 Prices have risen ... 10% over the past few months.

G *Strike out the wrong sentence:*

1. a/ What time is it?   b/ What time it is?
2. a/ I don't know what time is it.
   b/ I don't know what time it is.
3. a/ What the matter is with you?
   b/ What is the matter with you?
4. a/ I asked him what was the matter with him.
   b/ I asked him what the matter was with him.
5. a/ What did he say?   b/ What he said?
6. a/ I really don't know what did he say.
   b/ I really don't know what he said.
7. a/ Will the Smiths come?   b/ The Smiths will come?
8. a/ He doesn't know whether will the Smiths come.
   b/ He doesn't know whether the Smiths will come.
9. a/ How did you do this?   b/ How you did it?
10. a/ He told me how you did it.
    b/ He told me how did you do it.
11. a/ When you are going to London?
    b/ When are you going to London?
12. a/ He asked me when you were going to London.
    b/ He asked me when were you going to London.
13. a/ Whose car is this?   b/ Whose car this is?
14. a/ How could we know whose car is this?
    b/ How could we know whose car this is?
15. a/ Where will they spend their holidays?
    b/ Where they will spend their holidays?
16. a/ I have not the slightest idea of where will they spend their holidays.
    b/ I have not the slightest idea of where they will spend their holidays.
17. a/ Why did he do this?   b/ Why he did this?
18. a/ I wonder why he did this.
    b/ I wonder why did he do this.
19. a/ What do you want to know?   b/ What you want to know?
20. a/ Tell me what you want to know.
    b/ Tell me what do you want to know.

Test

1 He endeavoured ... to their rescue.
- a/ to go
- b/ go
- c/ going
- d/ gone

2 What had they intended ...?
- a/ do
- b/ doing
- c/ done
- d/ to do

3 When the truth was found out, he turned out ... a crook.
- a/ be
- b/ to be
- c/ having been
- d/ being

4 Couldn't you avoid ... such mistakes?
- a/ make
- b/ to make
- c/ making
- d/ made

5 I hope they won't mind ... .
- a/ that we come
- b/ us coming
- c/ we coming
- d/ our coming

6 They are said ... extremely nice people.
- a/ be
- b/ to be
- c/ being
- d/ been

7 Why did he reproach ...?
- a/ to you that you went
- b/ you to have gone
- c/ you with going
- d/ at you to go

8 I've been told that he is charged ... his wife.
- a/ with killing
- b/ for killing
- c/ to have killed
- d/ of having killed

9 Don't try not to tell ... me the truth.
- a/ —
- b/ at
- c/ to
- d/ for

10 What did he say ... you ... her?
- a/ — / off
- b/ at / of
- c/ to / about
- d/ — / about

11 Do you really believe you can dispense ... foreign languages?
- a/ —
- b/ of
- c/ off
- d/ with

12 At least you should bear in mind that, nowadays, people cannot do ... English.
- a/ without
- b/ until
- c/ out of
- d/ with

13 Very few people attended ... his lecture.
- a/ at
- b/ in
- c/ with
- d/ —

14 That country's population has risen ... 3 % over the past decade.
- a/ by
- b/ of
- c/ in
- d/ off

15 Aren't you interested ... anything at all?
- a/ by
- b/ at
- c/ in
- d/ of

16 Why did you disagree ... him?
- a/ at
- b/ with
- c/ upon
- d/ —

17 Have you finally agreed ... a common policy?
- a/ at
- b/ with
- c/ upon
- d/ for

18 Do you happen to know where ...?
- a/ live they
- b/ do they live
- c/ have they lived
- d/ they live

19 I doubt whether ....
- a/ they'll come at all
- b/ will they come at all
- c/ shall they come at all
- d/ come they at all

20 People are convinced that they must keep up ... the Joneses.
- a/ to
- b/ with
- c/ for
- d/ at

A FEW PROBLEMS OF THE CONTEMPORARY WORLD

A *Translate into English:*

1 Le but de la publicité est de vendre aux consommateurs.
2 C'est pourquoi elle doit à tout prix attirer l'attention des gens.
3 Son but est d'éviter de choquer les gens.
4 Il faut éviter la saturation des marchés et créer des débouchés pour les produits.
5 La qualité de leurs marchandises n'a cessé de baisser au cours de ces dernières années.
6 Pour défendre les consommateurs il reste beaucoup à faire.
7 Les Américains disent que Nader est très efficace.
8 On dit qu'il est très efficace.
9 Nous devons forcer les gens à consommer de plus en plus.
10 On force les gens à acheter plus qu'ils ne voudraient.
11 On dit que la pollution est responsable de certains cancers du poumon.
12 Les responsables laissent trop souvent les industriels polluer notre environnement.
13 Nous devons amener les gouvernements à prendre des mesures.
14 Il a réussi à faire appliquer la loi.
15 Le nombre de cancers du poumon est deux fois plus élevé dans les villes que dans les campagnes.

B *Translate into English:*

1 Je me rappelle avoir vu cette rivière pleine de poissons; maintenant, elle charrie de la boue industrielle.
2 Je ne dois pas oublier d'assister à la réunion demain.
3 Cet homme dit qu'il a vu le voleur attraper le sac à main de cette dame.
4 On l'a vu attraper le sac à main de cette dame.
5 Je n'oublierai jamais le fait qu'ils ont refusé de nous aider à sortir de nos difficultés.
6 Les pays qui souffrent de la famine espèrent que les pays riches vont leur fournir de la nourriture.
7 Ils ne s'attendaient pas à ce que le gouvernement prenne des mesures pour diminuer la pollution.
8 Si nous continuons à gaspiller le pétrole, les réserves seront épuisées avant l'an 2000.

C *Translate into English:*

1. On leur a reproché de ne pas avoir pris de mesures pour limiter la croissance de la population.
2. Ils nous ont confié leurs enfants pour une semaine.
3. On a envoyé chercher le docteur.
4. On lui a offert quelques très jolis cadeaux pour son anniversaire.
5. Vous ne devriez pas leur cacher vos difficultés.
6. On l'accuse d'avoir pris des mesures trop sévères.
7. Je crois qu'il a emprunté beaucoup d'argent à son père.
8. Nous ne pouvons nous passer de vos services.
9. S'ils s'attaquent au problème de la surpopulation, ils rencontreront beaucoup de difficultés.
10. Je ne m'intéresse pas vraiment aux problèmes des pays riches.
11. Je voudrais commenter l'affirmation de l'auteur.
12. Nous dépendons entièrement des pays producteurs de pétrole.
13. Pourquoi a-t-il augmenté ses prix?
14. Les prix des produits alimentaires ont augmenté de 12 % cette année.
15. Les pays du Quart Monde ne peuvent se permettre d'acheter le pétrole à des prix aussi élevés.

D *Translate into English:*

1. Quelle est l'utilité de la publicité?
2. Je me demande quelle est l'utilité de la publicité.
3. Comment avez-vous l'intention de combattre la pollution ?
4. On m'a demandé comment j'avais l'intention de combattre la pollution.
5. A qui appartient cette maison?
6. Il m'a demandé à qui appartenait cette maison.
7. Intensifieront-ils la recherche nucléaire?
8. Je ne sais pas s'ils intensifieront la recherche nucléaire.
9. Où se trouve votre école?
10. On m'a demandé où se trouvait votre école.

Corrigés des exercices

Chap. I. Page 23 :

A 1 We usually watch television in the evening, but tonight John is reading and I am knitting.
2 Most young people wear jeans and T-shirts. Why are you wearing such a formal dress?
3 "Where are you going to?" "I'm going to the hairdresser's."
4 "Where do you spend the summer holidays?" "We always spend them in Italy."
5 "What are you thinking of?" "Of you and your stupid questions."
6 Do you always read a lot?
7 What are you reading right now?
8 Do you often buy sweets for the children?
9 The President addresses the nation every year. He is now speaking on television.
10 I take the bus to school every morning, but today my father is driving me.

B 1 "Who is knocking at the door?" "The milkman, I suppose."
2 What do you want to do tonight?
3 Do you agree with me?
4 The prima donna who lives next door is singing right now. Can you hear her?
5 I do not understand what you mean.
6 When he plays tennis, he always wears white shorts. Why is he wearing red ones today?
7 I always vote for the Democratic candidate.
8 I do not remember what happened that day.
9 "What do you think of our President?" "I think he does so little that he cannot possibly make many mistakes."
10 "What do they do on Saturday afternoons?" "They play baseball or soccer."

Page 24 :

A 1 went.
2 have been living.
3 have not spoken.
4 has been speaking.
5 went away.

CORRIGÉS DES EXERCICES

B
1. They have not written to us for a year.
2. That actress has not acted for ten years.
3. He has not been seen for a fortnight.
4. He has not spoken to her for six months.
5. They have not made a trip to London for two years.

Page 25 :

C
1. We have not had a party since John's birthday.
2. She has not called me on the phone since she was ill.
3. I have not read a detective novel since I was in hospital.
4. He has not given his son a present since the child was five.
5. We have not sent for the doctor since Mary had the flu.

D
1. It is three days since he last shaved.
2. It is two days since I last had a bite.
3. It is three years since Joan last spoke German.
4. It is three months since he last did any work.
5. It is six months since she last wrote to her mother.

E
1. a/ for   b/ since.
2. a/ since   b/ for.
3. a/ since   b/ for.
4. a/ for   b/ since.
5. a/ since   b/ for.

Page 27 :

A
1. was reading.
2. was writing.
3. attacked.
4. was planning.
5. heard.
6. was making.
7. burst.
8. was campaigning.
9. was looking at.
10. came in.

B
1. had been reading.
2. had not expected.
3. had left.
4. had had.
5. had been sitting.
6. had been living.
7. had been speaking.
8. had been told.
9. had been saving.
10. had been.

Page 28 :

A
1. for.
2. since.
3. for.
4. before.
5. ago.
6. for.
7. ago.
8. since.
9. ago; since.
10. before.

B | **1** Can you see John playing tennis?
2 Mr and Mrs Smith are sitting in their sitting-room: he is reading and she is playing the piano.
3 On Sundays they go for long walks.
4 They have been married for 20 years.
5 They got married 20 years ago.
6 When I got acquainted with the Wilsons, their son had been dead for 3 months.
7 He had been killed in a car-crash 3 months before.
8 "What do you do on leaving your office?" "I usually go shopping but today I'm going home."
9 They have been talking politics for an hour.
10 John arrived an hour ago; since then he has been playing with my little boy.
11 They lived in this neighbourhood ten years ago, but now they live in a distant (=remote) suburb.
12 How long have you been living in this house?

Page 29 :

C | **1** That Indian has been working as a window-cleaner for 2 years.
2 He had an accident 3 months ago.
3 He had never been subject to vertigo before, but (ever) since he fell he has been afraid of taking risks.
4 For a few years (some) movements have been claiming a better status for the Indians.
5 When the Pilgrim Fathers arrived, the Indians had been living in America for centuries.
6 Two centuries ago, the Americans had to fight to obtain their independence.
7 When Independence War broke out, the Americans had had nothing to fear from France and Spain for some time.
8 When she arrived in America, her husband had been living there for 3 years.
9 They had been separated for 3 years.
10 They had not seen each other (ever) since he had left their native country.

D | **1** That man had been having a leisurely way of life (ever) since he had migrated to a Southern state.
2 The American troops had been suffering set-backs for about two years when Lafayette arrived.
3 Morgan had felt attracted by the Frontier for a long time when he decided to go west.
4 For how long had he been looking for gold when he found his first nugget?
5 How long ago did the Civil War take place?
6 How many years ago was he ruined by the crisis?

7 Since when have the Blacks been emancipated?
8 He had been unemployed for 8 months when he found this job.
9 For how long have you been (living) on the dole?
10 He was elected President a year ago; he has been governing the country for a year.

Pages 30 et 31 :

1 b.	**8** b.	**15** c.
2 a.	**9** c.	**16** a.
3 d.	**10** b.	**17** d.
4 d.	**11** c.	**18** c.
5 a.	**12** c.	**19** b.
6 d.	**13** d.	**20** a.
7 a.	**14** c.	

Chap. II. Page 47 :

A
1 find
2 doesn't improve
3 decide
4 gets
5 can
6 feel
7 gets
8 feel
9 come
10 is

B
1 were
2 could
3 had
4 were
5 worked
6 were
7 had found
8 had known
9 had had
10 had not read

Page 49 :

A
1 He writes in his letter that he'll try to get a job ...
2 The Wilsons keep saying that they'd like to go to California if they could afford the trip.
3 ... he keeps thinking how he'd like to be ...
4 She never stops saying that if she went to Hollywood she'd become ...
5 I usually tell her that she'd better give up her daydreaming .....

B
1 She wrote in her letter that they were doing very well ....
2 They told me that they had made such a lot of money from the sale of their cattle that they could hardly ....
3 She said that she would come if she must (= had to).
4 My brother wrote to me that they would like to go ....
5 Mrs Smith said to me that her little boy had just told her that he'd like to be a cowboy.
6 The teacher said that the mineral resources of Texas had made possible ....

CORRIGÉS DES EXERCICES

7 Peter Wilson wrote to me that he now had a very good job ....
8 The boss told me that we were going to build ....
9 The teacher said that cotton was the leading crop ....
10 Mary writes in her letter that she has bought ....
11 Mr. Pendleton told me that, if I didn't mind moving to another region, they could send me to Houston.
12 He added that they were opening ....

Page 51 :

A|
1 He asked us when we would go ....
2 The teacher asked who was going to ....
3 She asked us where we had spent our holidays.
4 He asked me why I had said that to Mary.
5 They asked us whether (= if) we would care to come to their party.
6 She asked what would happen if they didn't go.
7 John asked you whose book this was.
8 The child asked which way he should go.
9 Mary asked how you could say that to a child.
10 I asked her when she would be coming then.

B|
1 He said to her to come here at once.
2 She told him not to speak to her like that.
3 The gangster ordered that they (should) give him the money at once or he'd kill them all.
4 The judge said that they (should) bring in the defendant.
5 My mother told me not to bite my nails.

C|
1 ... I'd better work for my exam.
2 ... he'd better play a less brutal game.
3 ... he'd better pay the ransom ....
4 You'd better read a good book ....
5 ... I'd better stay at home.

Page 53 :

A|
1 The children were not allowed to watch television that night.
2 You were not allowed to apply for a government loan.
3 Our son was not allowed to enter Harvard.
4 I was not allowed to go to the theatre.
5 Pedestrians were not allowed to cross. ...

B|
1 a/ She should dress better.   b/ She ought to dress better.
2 a/ He should be less rude.   b/ He ought to be less rude.

3 a/ They should go to Florida.   b/ They ought to go to Florida.
4 a/ He should work better.   b/ He ought to work better.
5 a/ They should raise his salary. b/ They ought to raise....
6 a/ He should have told the truth. b/ He ought to have told....
7 a/ They should have been more.... b/ They ought to have been....
8 a/ They should have developed.... b/ They ought to have developped....

C
1. You needn't have spoken so rudely....
2. I didn't need to save money....
3. I needn't have saved so much money....
4. She needn't have spent so much time....
5. We didn't need to take the trip....
6. They needn't have taken....

Page 54 :

D
1. He'll enlarge his farm (stead) when he has obtained a loan.
2. Our daughter will settle down in the country as soon as she can.
3. When those pigs are fat enough we'll sell them.
4. If they hadn't mechanized their work, the Middle West farmers would obtain a lower yield.
5. If he didn't work on the assembly-line that factory-hand (= industrial worker) would be less unhappy.
6. If the quality of California wines hadn't improved they couldn't compete with French wines.

E
1. He says (that) he will settle down in San Francisco.
2. He keeps saying (that) he'd like to have a good job, but he doesn't work.
3. She says that, if her parents had been richer (= wealthier), she could have studied in Harvard.
4. He wrote to me that the crop would be bountiful this year.
5. They had said that they wouldn't stay here for a long time.
6. He explained to me that the lack of room checked San Francisco in its expansion (= growth).
7. That lovely young lady told me (that) she would love to go to Hollywood.
8. I asked that Texan how he had made a fortune.
9. I asked them whose ranch this was.
10. They asked me whether (= if) I'd like to go to the cinema to see a western.

CORRIGÉS DES EXERCICES

F| 1 His parents told him to stop talking (or: Her... told her).
2 The sheriff told the thieves to surrender.
3 Then he ordered that they (should) be hanged.
4 The engineer ordered that a new hole (should) be drilled.
5 He asked the driver to stop at a filling-station.

Page 55 :

G| 1 You'd better build apartment-buildings rather than office-buildings.
2 We'd rather (= sooner) live in a residential suburb than in the centre of Manhattan.
3 You'd better breed cattle rather than waste your time growing wheat.
4 They'd better not have listened to you.
5 I'd rather (= sooner) have sailed down the Mississippi than up stream: it would have been easier.

H| 1 They won't be able to come tomorrow.
2 They may be late.
3 May I borrow this book from you?
4 We might go to the East coast during the holidays.
5 The city must not expand too much.
6 They must have taken their car: it's not in their garage.
7 They told us that we should (= ought to) try to improve our production.
8 It was Mr Burns who said that to us: it ought to (= should) be a good piece of advice.

I| 1 He didn't need to come, so he stayed in San Francisco.
2 I needn't have called them (on the phone): they didn't listen to me.
3 You needn't have explained the situation to us: we had perfectly understood it.
4 I didn't need to talk, so I said nothing.

Pages 56-57 :

1 a.	8 b.	15 b.
2 b.	9 b.	16 b.
3 c.	10 c.	17 c.
4 d.	11 a.	18 d.
5 c.	12 a.	19 c.
6 b.	13 b.	20 b.
7 a.	14 a.	

Chap. III. Page 71 :

A
1. So will ours.
2. So might we.
3. So did John.
4. So can the Wilsons.
5. So will Joan.
6. So would I.
7. So has Mr Jones.
8. So do all working women.
9. So had all the women of her generation.
10. So should most women.

B
1. a/ Neither has Joan.
   b/ Joan hasn't either.
2. a/ Neither did Mrs Wilson.
   b/ Mrs Wilson didn't either.
3. a/ Neither should you.
   b/ You shouldn't either.
4. a/ Neither would I.
   b/ I wouldn't either.
5. a/ Neither would I.
   b/ I wouldn't either.
6. a/ Neither could I.
   b/ I couldn't either.
7. a/ Neither do most women.
   b/ Most women don't either.
8. a/ Neither had most Americans.
   b/ Most Americans hadn't either.
9. a/ Neither did you.
   b/ You didn't either.
10. a/ Neither will my wife.
    b/ My wife won't either.

Page 73 :

A
1. don't they?
2. isn't it?
3. didn't you?
4. haven't they?
5. couldn't he?
6. had she?
7. will they?
8. could she?
9. have you?
10. will it?

B
1. Never will leisure activities be accessible to ....
2. Not once did you go to ....
3. Not only can she look after ....
4. Little did she know ....
5. No sooner had she spoken than ....
6. Vainly have I tried ....
7. Nowhere are the children to be found.
8. Only when she is ready will we be able to leave.
9. So little pleasure did the party give them that ....
10. Never did I say such a thing.

CORRIGÉS DES EXERCICES 171

Page 75 :

A 1 b/ This detective novel is so interesting! c/ How interesting this detective novel is! d/ Isn't this detective novel interesting!
2 b/ What a devoted movie-goer Mary is! c/ Mary is such a devoted movie-goer!
3 b/ Their parties are always so formal! c/ How formal their parties always are! d/ Aren't their parties always formal!
4 b/ What an excellent actor he is! c/ He is such an excellent actor!
5 b/ What a widespread influence the mass media have! c/ The mass media have such a widespread influence!
6 b/ The freedom of the press is so important! c/ How important the freedom of the press is! d/ Isn't the freedom of the press important!
7 b/ What a nuisance TV commercials are! c/ TV commercials are such a nuisance!
8 b/ What (great) courage he showed in that ordeal! c/ He showed such (great) courage in that ordeal!

B 1 What an event ....
2 What a pity ....
3 ... such pity ....
4 What a stupid show ....
5 What a disgrace ....
6 What a lot of records ....
7 He is such a great musician! He has such talent!
8 ... such a beautiful negro spiritual!

Pages 76 et 77 :

1 a.	8 a.	15 d.
2 d.	9 c.	16 c.
3 b.	10 b.	17 c.
4 d.	11 b.	18 a.
5 a.	12 c.	19 a.
6 b.	13 b.	20 c.
7 c.	14 a.	

Pages 78 :

A 1 "I believe children are naturally good." "So do I."
2 She went to school until (= up to) the age of 18, and so did her brother.
3 "I must do my homework." "So must your brother."
4 "Peter would like to play tennis." "So would I."
5 "We can afford to send our children to college." "So can we."
6 When I left university, I had been studying (= attending classes) there for 6 years, and so had my husband.
7 "What is Mary doing now?" "She's working, and so is her brother."
8 "I'll attend Professor Wilson's lecture tomorrow." "So shall (= will) I."

9 My parents don't live with us, and neither do my parents-in-law (= and my parents-in-law don't either).
10 "She wouldn't like to give up her job for her husband." "Neither would I." (= "I wouldn't either.")
11 "We didn't have much money when we got married." "Neither did we." (= "We didn't either.").
12 "They are American but they weren't born in the U.S." "Neither were we." (= We weren't either.").

B | **1** Their children are well-bred, aren't they?
2 She has never contemplated working, has she?
3 When she got married she had never had a job, had she?
4 You'll take the car to go shopping, won't you?
5 Your husband has always liked pottering about the house, hasn't he?
6 There aren't many people who spend their leisure-time reading, are there?
7 If you had time, you'd read more, wouldn't you?
8 Your little boy is never bored, is he?

Page 79 :

C | **1** Never shall (= will) I buy a TV set.
2 Not only do they have no books at home, but they are proud of it.
3 Only in 1920 did jazz come to Chicago.
4 Not once did that singer sing (or: has that singer sung) without a mike.
5 Very seldom does a child of the underprivileged classes make bright studies.
6 He doesn't work well at school, nor is he very nice at home.
7 "On no account would I send my daughter to a coeducational school", the old lady said.
8 Never again will women accept to be their husbands' servants.
9 No sooner had they gone out for a walk than it started raining.
10 Nowhere are parties as nice as at the Martins'.
11 Never again shall I speak to him (or: her)!
12 Not only is he late, but he doesn't even apologize!

D | **1** What talent that (orchestra-) director has!
2 What a hurry you're in!
3 How pretty that song is!
4 What a lot of contemporaneous musicians live in the U.S.!
5 What relief to hear that the accident was not serious!
6 What a pity we can't go to that concert!
7 What a beautiful thing education is!
8 How sweet those children are!
9 What a disgrace for the family!
10 How low the level of studies is in that school!

CORRIGÉS DES EXERCICES

Chap. IV. Page 89 :

A|
1. What
2. what
3. which
4. what
5. which
6. which
7. What
8. what
9. which
10. What ... which
11. which
12. what

B|
1. My brother's house.
2. Keats'(s) life.
3. The Burts' car.
4. My aunt's friend's book.
5. It represents a week's work.
6. This is the Queen of England's crown.
7. This is Peter's and Jane's house.
8. He made a two hours' speech.
9. We spent the week-end at my uncle's.
10. I must go to the hairdresser's.
11. I didn't approve of Kennedy's, Johnson's and Nixon's policies.

Page 91 :

A|
1. her ... me
2. his ... mine ... yours
3. their ... them
4. me ... me
5. your ... yours
6. her ... hers
7. Mine
8. their ... theirs ... ours
9. us
10. its

B| (each other = one another):
1. each other
2. himself
3. yourself
4. each other
5. yourselves / yourself.
6. ourselves ... each other
7. yourself
8. herself
9. each other
10. yourself

Page 93 :

A|
1. I am shocked by his showing so much hypocrisy.
2. Do you mind her staying so late ?
3. Our going bankrupt surprised everybody.
4. Your gambling so recklessly will cause your ruin.
5. His mentioning the technological gap between ....
6. I'm sure they were annoyed by his arriving so late.
7. Their getting married so early was rather unexpected.
8. I was not surprised at her saying so.
9. She doesn't approve of his smoking so much.
10. Have you heard of their going to the States ?

B | **Since** expresses cause in the following sentences:
2 – 3 – 4 – 6 – 7 – 10.

Page 95 :

1 While	8 While	15 On
2 at	9 –, –	16 In / While
3 by	10 by	17 at
4 While / In	11 On	18 on
5 on	12 –, –	19 –, –
6 by	13 in / while	20 On
7 –	14 By	

Page 97 :

A |
1 much
2 Many
3 much
4 many
5 Many

B |
1 There are not as many self-made men in Europe as in the U.S.
2 There is not as much staff in their company as in ours.
3 Mr Smith has not as much influence on the workers as the other foremen.
4 They have not sold as many shares as yesterday.
5 They do not employ as many scientists as we do in our laboratory.
6 There are not as many workers on strike as last time.

C |
1 little, little
2 few
3 little
4 little
5 few

Pages 98 à 100 :

1 b.	8 b.	15 b.
2 c.	9 d.	16 d.
3 d.	10 a.	17 a.
4 c.	11 b.	18 d.
5 d.	12 d.	19 b.
6 c.	13 a.	20 c.
7 b.	14 b.	

CORRIGÉS DES EXERCICES

Page 101 :

A 1 According to some sociologists, what made for (= contributed to) the development of capitalism was Protestantism.
2 He thinks that work is a religious duty, which is a rather widespread attitude.
3 The Americans worship the Work Ethic, which accounts for the remarkable vitality of this country.
4 What you're putting forward is most interesting, but with what arguments do you support your theories?
5 What some consider as the Welfare State, others see as an inducement to laziness.
6 What this Director has just suggested might jeopardize our whole policy.
7 He believes in free enterprise, which is his right; I believe in government intervention, which is <u>my</u> right.
8 We are going to open a subsidiary (= a branch) in that country, which will enable us to capture the market.
9 What will enable us to capture the market is the complete lack of local industries.
10 The anti-trust laws are not always enforced, which is quite a pity (= regrettable).

B 1 It's my car, it's not John's, it's not yours, it's mine and nobody else's.
2 Here is your house, here is ours, here is the Wilsons', and over there is the Joneses' (house).
3 "You're sure this is Joan's bag?" "Since it's neither yours nor mine, it can only be hers."
4 Peter brought a dog; he said it was not his. Since it's neither yours nor that of our neighbours (= nor our neighbours'), we're going to keep it here.
5 Look at Mr and Mrs Wilson in their new car; they say it's theirs, but I think they've borrowed it.

Page 102 :

C 1 Those two firms keep competing (= vying) with each other (= one another).
2 They quarrelled for two hours before reaching an agreement.
3 Enjoy yourselves while you are young.
4 He loves himself and I adore myself: we get on very well.
5 Stop talking to each other (= one another), please.

D 1 His helping us was rather unexpected.
2 I don't approve at all of her smoking so much.
3 Their calling on us was a very pleasant surprise.
4 I'm very disappointed by his marrying such a dull girl.
5 Aren't you surprised by her going to this demonstration?

E 1 On getting home I saw that the children were not back.
2 The little girl went home crying because she did not like school.
3 Miss Smith earns a living (= a livelihood) by giving English lessons.
4 I was listening to the radio while reading the newspaper.
5 I am surprised at seeing that he has not followed my advice.
6 In flying to London I made the acquaintance of that charming old gentleman.

Page 103 :

F 1 She swam across the river.
2 We ran down the stairs.
3 He limped up the stairs.
4 They rode past the house.
5 They sailed out of the harbour.

Chap. V. Page 113 :

A 1 the most demanding
2 the best
3 the worst
4 the latest
5 the last
6 the worst-looking
7 the best-dressed
8 the eldest

B 1 I am as young as Peter.
2 We are as destitute as they (are).
3 You are as penniless as the Smiths.
4 Our house is as decrepit as theirs.
5 Traffickers are as dangerous as pushers.

C 1 Their house is not so pleasant as ours.
2 Your children are not so rebellious as the Joneses'.
3 Mary is not so plain as her elder sister.
4 Your living conditions are not so bad as those of ... .
5 The wages of the Blacks are not so high as those of ... .

Page 115 :

A 1 Prices are higher and higher.
2 The children go to bed later and later.
3 My health is worse and worse.
4 This leader is more and more popular.
5 Holiday-makers have to go farther and farther to ... .
6 ... the poor are more and more destitute.

B 1 The better I know him, the less I like him.
2 The better acquainted we get, the nicer I find her.
3 The sooner you come, the happier we'll be.
4 The more he drinks, the worse he looks.
5 The farther you go, the more things you'll see.
6 The older we get, the better-off we are.

C 1 The inequities they see in their society make some young Americans rebel.
2 Despair made him commit a robbery.
3 Drug-addiction made him become a criminal.
4 A pusher made him become a drug-addict.
5 The arrival of the police patrol made the mugger flee.
6 You make me find life more pleasant.

Page 117 :

A 1 are used to living
2 used to live
3 are used to being
4 used to ill-treat
5 used to be
6 are used to locking
7 used to denounce
8 am used to living

B 1 The room is too noisy for me to work in peace.
2 Those prejudices are too deep-rooted for us to eradicate them.
3 The American Whites are too prejudiced for desegregation to be achieved.
4 The gangsters proved too shrewd for the police to arrest them.
5 He is too inveterate a drug-addict for the doctor to save him.
6 The car went too fast for me to see the faces of ... .

C 1 whatever
2 whenever
3 Whoever
4 whichever
5 Wherever
6 whatever

Pages 118 et 119 :

1 d.
2 c.
3 a.
4 c.
5 b.
6 b.
7 b.
8 a.
9 d.
10 a.
11 c.
12 b.
13 c.
14 d.
15 d.
16 a.
17 c.
18 a.

Page 120 :

A 1 I find their situation as interesting as yours.
2 The poor Whites' children are not quite as destitute as the poor Blacks' children.
3 They are not as politically active as we are.
4 The young Americans' rebellion is not as violent as before.
5 He is the least active man I know.
6 He is (all) the more destitute as he is now jobless.
7 He is very destitute, (all) the more so as (= especially as) he is now unemployed.
8 They are (all) the poorer as they have been affected by the crisis.
9 Those workers' wages are (all) the lower as they are illegal immigrants.
10 He is (all) the less excusable as he belongs to a privileged class.
11 The people who question the Work Ethic are more and more numerous.
12 The more there are, the better it is.
13 Drug-addicts are unfortunately more and more numerous.
14 The less there are, the better it is.
15 The poorer their parents are, the less chances they have of carrying on their studies.

D 1 I've had my hair cut.
2 We had the elderly helped.
3 Make him come to my office.
4 It was he who made me take drugs for the first time.
5 They make the unemployed wait for hours.
6 Our neighbours (have) had their old dilapidated house repaired.
7 The American withdrawal from Vietnam made the students' rebellion abate somewhat (= caused the students' rebellion to abate somewhat).

Page 121 :

C 1 They are used to demonstrating when they are not satisfied.
2 The Blacks are used to living in decaying slums.
3 When he was a child, he used to loaf about the streets all day.
4 Unskilled workers are used to receiving ridiculously low wages.
5 City-dwellers are now used to witnessing hold-ups in the United States.
6 They used to dwell (= live) in residential districts when they were young.

D 1 He is too old now for me to find him a job.
2 The neighbourhood is too poor for the schools to be improved.
3 They are too numerous for us to (be able to) defeat them.
4 That criminal is too hardened for us to hope to save him.
5 That school is too mediocre for our children to attend it.
6 That tie is too ugly for you to wear it tonight.

7 There are too many thefts (= robberies) in the city for the inhabitants to feel safe at night.
8 It is too late for her to walk back home on her own.

E **1** Wherever you may go, whatever you may do, you cannot avoid these people.
2 However numerous you may be, you'll be welcome.
3 Whoever did that deserves a reward.
4 Take whichever of these books if you're interested in them.
5 Come whenever you like.
6 However young he may be, he has no excuse for having behaved in this manner.

Chap. VI. Page 131 :

1 ...was almost unlimited.
2 ...the U.S. had just entered ....
3 ...was not quite ready.
4 Even the Americans ....
5 ...was completely destroyed ....
6 ...progressed slowly but steadily.
7 ...the marines usually stormed ....
8 ...was already reconquered.
9 { On June 6, 1944, the Allied forces ...
     { ...on the shores of Normandy, on June 6, 1944.
10 ...the U.S. { should never have used ....
              { should have never used ....
11 I am hardly ever tired.
12 There were not enough dug-outs ...
13 ...you have not worked enough ....
14 He is not old enough to see that film.
15 NATO was also created ....
16 We very much appreciated ... (complément long).
17 We enjoyed that film very much. (complément court).
18 The Cuban missile crisis nearly led to a war.
19 ...was officially conducted by ...
20 Unfortunately he was killed ...
21 He'll receive you at ten o'clock tomorrow.
22 The Presidency no longer enjoys ....
23 ...Kennedy increased substantially ....
              substantially increased ...
24 ...has deeply scarred ....
25 ...are now experiencing ....

Page 133 :

A| 1 The Allied forces kept receiving military aid from the U.S..
   2 The numerous weapons sent to Great Britain were a substantial help.
   3 a/ The obvious aim of Japan was to dominate Eastern Asia.
      b/ The aim of Japan to dominate Eastern Asia was obvious.
   4 The U.S. did not play { a merely passive / merely a passive } part in the war.
   5 There are far too many Americans who think that the atomic bomb should have been used in Vietnam.

B| 1 The atomic bomb is a horrific weapon.
   2 He is a salesman very polite with customers.
   3 The Princess Royal was present at their party.
   4 { A pretty young woman, well-dressed and well-spoken ....
      A pretty, well-dressed, well-spoken young woman .... }
   5 Look at our children asleep in their little beds.
   6 We must not wake up those sleeping children.
   7 Give me a list of the goods available.
   8 Have you ever read a prettier story?
   9 I know he is a man kind to his fellow-men.
   10 The mere thought of ....
   11 They are the nicest people alive.
   12 { Intelligent though he may be, ...
      Though he may be intelligent, ... }
   13 Experience makes men wise.
   14 She is a woman envious of other people.
   15 The lane is only three feet wide.
   16 My brother is a man jealous of the people who work with him.
   17 Did they announce anything new on the radio?
   18 I don't mind living and dying alone.

Page 134 :

A| 1 In <u>the</u> United States <u>the</u> conflict between <u>the</u> Blacks and <u>the</u> Whites is by no means over.
   2 In <u>the</u> South, white people have always protested against desegregation.
   3 Slavery was abolished over a century ago.
   4 ... "Black is beautiful."
   5 <u>The</u> blue of your dress is lovely.
   6 English is not a difficult language.
   7 <u>The</u> English they speak in America is different from <u>the</u> English spoken by <u>the</u> British.
   8 <u>The</u> influence of Protestantism over (<u>the</u>) Americans ....

CORRIGÉS DES EXERCICES

9 The importance attached to education and leisure testifies to the development of a society.
10 ... suffering from poverty and unemployment.
11 The unemployment now prevailing ... .
12 I listen to the radio, I go to the cinema, I use the telephone and I read the press. But I do not watch television.
13 Queen Elizabeth I played a major role in British history (= in the history of Britain).
14 The President delivered ... .
15 ... the Police, the Army or the Navy ... .

Page 135 :

B | 1 I read a detective novel and a science fiction one, and I liked both.
2 The novel is the most popular literary genre.
3 Business is business.
4 The dog is the friend of man.
5 ... to understand women.
6 ... in England.
7 The England I love is the England of the 18th century, rural England.
8 Baldwin, a Black writer of talent, helps us to understand the reactions of (the) American Blacks.
9 Rebellion and violence are manifestations of a / the moral crisis in America.
10 We play tennis on Sundays.
11 He always speaks the truth.
12 Last year, I went to America, and next year, I'll go to Africa. I'm interested in both continents.
13 What a pity you cannot come to the States with me!
14 What contempt the Whites show for the Blacks!
15 When I was a child, the President, a very simple man, came to our city.
16 The mass media have such (an) influence on the silent majority!
17 ... as important a problem for us as it is for you.
18 I'll be ready in half an hour.
19 ... twice a month.
20 (The) Americans have a guilty conscience where the Blacks and the Indians are concerned.
21 He's got a headache and a sore throat: he must have the flu.
22 Considering what (the) wages are in this country, the workers have a right to complain.
23 The English are said to have a sense of humour.
24 I'm at a loss as to how to put an end to this affair.
25 Teenagers must study modern languages.

Page 137 :

A
1. She is beaten ...
2. The story was begun ...
3. Their prisoner is being bound to a tree.
4. The table has been broken.
5. A house is being built.
6. An award had been given to him = He had been given an award.
7. A letter was sent to ... = Their parents were sent a letter.
8. English is taught to the pupils = The pupils are taught English.
9. A story is told to ... = Her children are told a story.
10. This attitude can't be put up with.
11. The chairs were taken away.
12. The children are often kept in.
13. What the lecturer said was being put down.
14. The bottle was flung violently.
15. The problem has been thought over.
16. Your letter has been read through carefully.
17. Amazing arguments were put forward to convince us.
18. A lot of fruit is eaten in summer.
19. She is found very pretty.
20. They were being spoken to in a very rude manner.

B
1. Like
2. as
3. as
4. as
5. as
6. like
7. like
8. like
9. like
10. as — as.

Pages 138 à 140 :

1. d.
2. b.
3. a.
4. a.
5. b.
6. d.
7. d.
8. b.
9. c.
10. d.
11. b.
12. b.
13. c
14. c.
15. a.
16. d.
17. b.
18. c.
19. a.
20. b.

Page 141 :

A
1. The Americans tested the atomic bomb only once before using it in Japan.
2. The bomb had never been used before.
3. Almost immediately after, the Japanese capitulated.
4. The Japanese were not the only ones to be horrified.

CORRIGÉS DES EXERCICES

    5 Have you ever heard of biological weapons?
    6 They had never heard of them.
    7 Casualties (= Losses in men) are always heavy in a war { such as WW II. / like WW II.
    8 An attack has never been checked in such a way (= manner).
    9 The town was altogether (= completely, entirely) destroyed by bombings.
  10 They had already bombed half the country.

B | **1** They are always prepared (= ready) to fight whoever might attack them.
    2 I'm always surprised when I hear such assertions (= statements).
    3 Aren't you ever afraid when you see what awful weapons are produced?
    4 Let us never be too pessimistic!
    5 I'm always thirsty during (the) meals.

C | **1** We're leaving for the U.S. the day after tomorrow.
    2 They happened to meet (They met by chance) at some friends' the day before yesterday.
    3 I had been entirely convinced by their arguments.
    4 We liked this film very much.
    5 They didn't very much like that book relating the life of an American family during the war.

Page 142 :

D | **1** We never have enough money to make (both) ends meet.
    2 They didn't have enough soldiers to defend themselves.
    3 You're not optimistic enough.
    4 But <u>he</u> is too pessimistic.
    5 I've too much work.
    6 Too many soldiers were killed.
    7 They are not determined enough.
    8 They did not take a decision quickly enough.

E | **1** He was not a remarkable president.
    2 That war was particularly cruel.
    3 The CIA has remained powerful and its interventions excessive.
    4 I've seen nothing remarkable in that man.
    5 Yet he is said to have done something surprising.
    6 Have you ever seen a more interesting film?
    7 There's something wrong.
    8 He was declared guilty.

184 CORRIGÉS DES EXERCICES

F | **1** There are people asleep in this room.
2 I like to walk alone (= to go for walks alone).
3 Look at that boat adrift on the river.
4 He was lying awake on his bed.
5 She is a woman jealous of the beauty of other women.
6 She is a jealous wife.
7 The room is 30 feet long by 20 feet wide.
8 That story is several centuries old.

Page 143 :

G | **1** They were killed by the enemy.
2 They are said to have been killed by the enemy.
3 I've been told (that) you intended to resign.
4 He had been told (that) his popularity would be increased.
5 I've been told something very funny.
6 The presidential myth was tarnished by that scandal.
7 Cuba was not reconquered by the exiles who landed in 1961.
8 A new weapon was being developed.
9 The island was being invaded.
10 The Philippines were being reconquered.

H | **1** We live like Americans. We live as in America.
2 I am young and hard-working like him (= as he is).
3 She was charming and well-bred like her sister (= as was her sister).
4 I'm going to react like you (= as you did) to their proposal.
5 I'll do as you like.

Chap. VII. Pages 154 à 158 :

A | **1** to talk
2 to be
3 to attend
4 call
5 to do
6 to solve
7 leave
8 stay
9 work
10 to do
11 to see
12 to take
13 to help
14 have
15 say

B | **1** say − to say
2 do
3 to be
4 to come
5 to be
6 to arrive
7 to buy
8 to write
9 to drink
10 to swim
11 to take
12 speak
13 know − to come
14 jump
15 to jump
16 shout
17 to shout
18 sing
19 to sing
20 to hand in

CORRIGÉS DES EXERCICES

C
1. to look after
2. making
3. saying
4. doing
5. to do
6. to stay
7. taking
8. to send
9. helping
10. being
11. flying
12. having
13. to raise
14. walking
15. disappear
16. to be
17. to succeed
18. singing
19. to do
20. flying-sailing

D
1. at.
2. ...
3. for
4. ...; with (or: for)
5. from
6. ...; to
7. ...; to
8. ...; to
9. on
10. ...; with
11. ...; with
12. for
13. with
14. of
15. for
16. with
17. of
18. on
19. from
20. from

E
1. with
2. on
3. for
4. of
5. with
6. in
7. on (= upon)
8. with
9. of
10. for
11. of
12. ...
13. at; to
14. on (= upon)
15. on (= upon)

F
1. in
2. ...; for
3. on (= upon)
4. with; for
5. upon
6. in
7. in
8. over
9. on
10. to
11. ...
12. ...
13. ...
14. to
15. by

G The right sentences are:
1. a
2. b
3. b
4. b
5. a
6. b
7. a
8. b
9. a
10. a
11. b
12. a
13. a
14. b
15. a
16. b
17. a
18. a
19. a
20. a

CORRIGÉS DES EXERCICES

Pages 159 et 160 :

1 a	**8** a	**15** c
2 d	**9** a	**16** b
3 b	**10** c	**17** c
4 c	**11** d	**18** d
5 d	**12** a	**19** a
6 b	**13** d	**20** b
7 c	**14** a	

Page 161 :

A
1. The aim of advertising is to sell to consumers.
2. This is why it must draw people's attention at any cost.
3. Its aim is to avoid shocking people.
4. Glutted markets must be avoided and outlets for the products must be created.
5. The quality of their goods has kept decreasing (or: deteriorating) over the past years.
6. There remains much to be done to defend consumers.
7. (The) Americans say (that) Nader is very efficient.
8. He is said to be very efficient.
9. We must { push people to consume / make people consume } more and more.
10. People are made to buy more than they'd like to.
11. Pollution is said to be responsible for some lung cancers.
12. The authorities too often let the industrialists (or: manufacturers) pollute our environment.
13. We must get the governments to take measures.
14. He succeeded in enforcing the law.
15. The lung cancer rate is twice as high in the cities as in the country.

B
1. I remember seeing this river teeming with (= full of) fish; now it carries industrial wastes.
2. I must remember (= I mustn't forget) to attend the meeting tomorrow.
3. That man says he saw the thief snatch that lady's purse.
4. He was seen to snatch that lady's purse.
5. I'll never forget (=I'll always remember) their refusing (=that they refused) to help us out of our difficulties.
6. The countries suffering from starvation hope that the rich nations will supply them with food.
7. They weren't expecting (or: They didn't expect) the government to take measures (in order) to reduce (=to curb) pollution.
8. If we go on wasting oil, the reserves will be exhausted by the year 2000.

Page 162

C 1 They've been reproached with not having taken measures to curb population growth.
2 They've entrusted us with their children for a week.
3 The doctor has been (or: was) sent for.
4 He (or: She) has been presented with (= given) some very pretty gifts for his (or: her) birthday.
5 You shouldn't conceal (= hide) your difficulties from them.
6 He is charged with (= accused of) having taken too strict measures.
7 I think he borrowed a lot of money from his father.
8 We can't do without (= dispense with) your services.
9 If they tackle the problem of overpopulation, they'll meet with many (= a lot of) difficulties.
10 I'm not really interested in the problems of rich nations.
11 I'd like to comment on (= upon) the author's assertion.
12 We are entirely dependent upon (= We entirely depend upon) the oil-producing nations.
13 Why did he raise his prices?
14 Food prices have risen by twelve per cent over the past year.
15 (The) Fourth World countries can't afford to buy oil at such high prices.

D 1 What use is advertising?
2 I wonder what use advertising is.
3 How do you intend to fight pollution?
4 I've been asked how I intended to fight pollution.
5 Whose house is that?
6 He asked me whose house that was.
7 Will they intensify nuclear research?
8 I don't know whether they'll intensify nuclear research.
9 Where is your school?
10 I've been asked where your school was.

Table des matières

- *Comment utiliser cet aide-mémoire* 3
- *Expressions utiles pour le commentaire de texte* . 4

I. THE MAKING OF AMERICA

The Indians 6
Colonial America 8
Independence War 10
The Frontier 12
The Civil War 14
The Melting-pot 16
The Crisis of 1929 and the New Deal 18
How American democracy works 20
- *Grammar and exercises* 22

II. THE MAIN REGIONS OF THE UNITED STATES

New England 32
New York and the Megalopolis 34
The Middle West 36
The Mississippi 38
California 40
Texas 42
The South 44
- *Grammar and exercises* 46

III. MODERN AMERICA

Education 58
The American family 60
American women 62
Leisure 64
The mass media 66
Music 68
- *Grammar and exercises* 70

IV. THE AFFLUENT SOCIETY

Protestantism and the Work Ethic 80
Business 82
Wall Street 84
Industry 86
- *Grammar and exercises* 88

V. THE SEAMY SIDE OF THE AFFLUENT SOCIETY

Poverty and unemployment	104
Rebellion	106
Crime, violence and drugs	108
The colour problem	110
— *Grammar and exercises*	112

VI. THE UNITED STATES IN THE WORLD

The U.S. and World War II	122
The American leadership and the cold war	124
J. F. Kennedy: myth and reality	126
The Vietnam war	128
— *Grammar and exercises*	130

VII. A FEW PROBLEMS OF THE CONTEMPORARY WORLD

The consumer society	144
Environment and pollution	146
Population growth	148
Hunger in the world	150
The energy crisis	152
— *Grammar and exercises*	154
Corrigés des exercices	163

Imprimé en France par
BRODARD GRAPHIQUE — Coulommiers-Paris
10/5632/2.
Dépôt légal n° 0959, 5-1980.

Collection n° 17
Édition n° 04

16/4683/5